Praise for *Love over Fear*

Dan White Jr. is an articulate practitioner who, in this much-needed book, exposes the toxic pathology of our current political climate. Jesus followers must resist the siren calls coming from every quarter of the culture and stand secure in the unshakable kingdom that Dan both embodies and ushers in. *Love over Fear* is a wake-up call!

ALAN HIRSCH
Author and founder of 100 Movements, 5Q Collective, and Forge International

Dan White Jr. has aptly diagnosed—we cannot heal our divides until we've confessed our fears, cannot overcome fear until we've committed to love. With fascinating cultural artifacts and compelling biblical stories, *Love over Fear* enriches our imagination for love, not as sentiment, but as the embodied, patient practice of embracing the other. I have great hope that with this book in hand, we the church can begin to move beyond "Us" and "Them" into our healing role as the people of God.

JEN POLLOCK MICHEL
Author of *Surprised by Paradox, Keeping Place,* and *Christianity Today*'s 2015 Book of the Year, *Teach Us to Want*

In each epic of history, social issues frame the way of being the church in the world. In *Love over Fear*, Dan White Jr. is a careful guide through the challenges and opportunities facing ordinary people. With brilliant nuance, he gives a pathway of faithful witness both personally and as a movement.

HUGH HALTER
Author of *Tangible Kingdom, Flesh,* and *Brimstone*

By unmasking the ferocious fear that divides us, Dan helps us to see our enemies as people, not monsters. He puts real flesh on the kind of love that can heal us. He passionately reminds us that truth and love is found in a person—Jesus, the One who embodies a limitless love that has the power to create family from enemies. This is a book for our polarized times!

JR WOODWARD
Author *Creating a Missional Culture*; coauthor, *The Church as Movement*; National Director, V3 movement

Is your soul fatigued by our polarized world? *Love over Fear* will breathe oxygen into your lungs and speak hope into your ears. Simple yet profound, vulnerable but strong, grounded in the words and ways of Jesus, and full of wonderful stories, Dan White Jr.'s book is the help we need for these troubled times.

DAVID FITCH
Northern Seminary; author of *The Church of Us vs. Them*

What a highly practical and hope-filled book Dan White Jr. has given us! *Love over Fear* disrupts our deep tendency to be polarized while offering us a unique path forward toward healing. This desperately needed and timely message dives into the life of Jesus for real ways we can continue the work of reconciliation today. *Love over Fear* is a gift to all God's people.

BRUXY CAVEY
Teaching Pastor at The Meeting House; author of *(Re)Union*

LOVE OVER FEAR

FACING MONSTERS, BEFRIENDING ENEMIES, AND HEALING OUR POLARIZED WORLD

DAN WHITE JR.

MOODY PUBLISHERS

CHICAGO

Edited by Connor Sterchi
Interior design: Ragont Design
Cover design: Erik M. Peterson
Author photo: Tonya Variya

All websites and phone numbers listed herein are accurate at the time of publication, but may change in the future or cease to exist. The listing of website references and resources does not imply publisher endorsement of the site's entire contents. Groups and organizations are listed for informational purposes, and listing does not imply publisher endorsement of their activities.

Names: White, Dan, Jr., author.
Title: Love over fear : facing monsters, befriending enemies, and healing our
  polarized world / Dan White Jr.
Description: Chicago : Moody Publishers, 2019. | Includes bibliographical
  references.
Identifiers: LCCN 2019012286 (print) | LCCN 2019004719 (ebook) | ISBN
  9780802418883 | ISBN 9780802497604 ()
Subjects: LCSH: Fear--Religious aspects--Christianity. | Love--Religious
  aspects--Christianity.
Classification: LCC BV4908.5 .W545 2019 (ebook) | LCC BV4908.5 (print) | DDC
  248.4--dc23
LC record available at https://lccn.loc.gov/2019012286

ISBN: 978-0-8024-1888-3

We hope you enjoy this book from Moody Publishers. Our goal is to provide high-quality, thought-provoking books and products that connect truth to your real needs and challenges. For more information on other books and products written and produced from a biblical perspective, go to www.moodypublishers.com or write to:

Moody Publishers
820 N. LaSalle Boulevard
Chicago, IL 60610

1 3 5 7 9 10 8 6 4 2

Printed in the United States of America

Tonya, my love, you have invited me
to swim in the current of kenosis.
This book is inspired by you.

CONTENTS

FOREWORD

Few can dismiss that we are now living in a time of profound upheaval. Experts call the era we are experiencing VUCA; one that is volatile, uncertain, complex, and ambiguous. These four conditions combine to create a situation of mass anxiety, the kind of which we (at least for those of us living in the West) have not experienced for a long, long time. The last time we experienced significant levels of VUCA was probably between the two world wars, and it accelerated the ideologically driven search for a stable moral and social order. This resulted in the rise of totalitarian rule in the USSR as well as the national socialism in Germany. The net result was World War II. There are real similarities to our current times; we are living in instability because everything is now wired and connected, and now fear can go viral.

I experience this as I travel across North America, Europe, and Australia: I listen to the stories of local church leaders trying to navigate increasingly complex situations. Take for instance our German friends trying to be a presence for Christ to both Syrian refugees and the hostile locals who want them kicked out of the country. Even in beautiful Sweden there is the rise of both the alt-right and alt-left groups as well as

Muslim extremism. All over Europe, racial, political and religious divides are being drawn. Fear of "the other" is growing out of control. There is an alarming rise in hate crimes, motivated by ideology, cropping up throughout the US. Things are definitely heating to a boiling point. Where there was once differences, there is now pure disgust. My husband—of European Jewish origin and raised in racist South Africa—knows what rabid political ideology looks and feels like—is having real premonitions of war. It might be his prophetic intuitions, or he might just be having too much cheese in his food at night, but he does sense something. Do you feel it too?

And these are just the macro, global trends. Similar forces are being played out on a personal and micro level. Just think about the profoundly polarizing effect that social media is having on all of us. We now find ourselves, whether we like it or not, personally swept up into the vortex of VUCA. It's not hard to see these forces at work. Everyone with a vague notion of anything and with a whole lot of *angst* can unleash their oft-times mean-spirited (even dangerous) words. It's almost as if our statements made on social media don't have significance unless they cut someone just a little. And of course, we all have our news sources and facts to back up our beliefs and behaviors. Ordinary Christians are caught in this boxing match. We are polarized against our friends, our families, and our neighbors. I have to take regular breaks from social media because it makes me anxious and robs me of my peace. Sometimes I think I can even smell the contagion of fear that leaks out from Facebook and Twitter . . . who needs this in their life?

But there is a reason for all this fear, and there is a real solution to be found. The Scriptures clearly explain the roots of human fear that lead to anger, that lead to agonizing drama throughout. For Christians, these things should come as no surprise. But somehow Christians have been caught in the undertow of our current tidal wave of fear. The Scriptures also tell of the words, works, and ways of Jesus. This changes everything and points all things in the right direction. Where love triumphs over fear! But I will leave Dan to tell you that good news of this particular love that exists beyond all ideology.

The world around us is aching for an alternative; Dan can feel it. With a tender heart and a tangible urgency, Dan calls God's people to step beyond their fear to experience the defining Christian form of love to which all followers of Jesus are called—to the love of our neighbor and even to our enemy. Believe it or not, this message is revolutionary. We need wisdom for this revolution, and Dan is sage in such matters. You will be comforted throughout, but he will also bring you consternation. He knows how tough it is to be a disciple in these complex times, but he also knows first-hand the supernatural power love has over fear.

There is never a better time than the present to give love a fighting chance.

DEBRA HIRSCH
Cofounder of Forge Mission Training
Author of *Redeeming Sex* and coauthor of *Untamed*

INTRODUCTION

A few years back I had two separate events occur in the same month that stirred up a storm within me. First, I had an individual who attends my church, someone dear to me, decide to leave. The circumstances around her departure left me scratching my head. She gently shared with me, "Dan, I don't feel safe in this church knowing there are liberals here who believe so differently than me. I just can't relax and be myself." I tried desperately to communicate safety and that there was space for her, but it wasn't enough.

Fast forward just a couple of weeks later; a couple came to me with the same intense concern, yet this time from the opposite angle. "Dan, we're not sure we will ever feel settled here with people who hold such conservative positions. We need a church that takes sides on these types of issues." I tried to persuade them that our church was a space for both conservatives and progressives to dwell in community together. They made it clear they'd be looking for a truly progressive church. I grieved that both of these folks could not stay in the mix together. They were repelled by each other. Rather than moving toward one another, despite their differences, they chose separation. I sense this moment was a snapshot of the state of our country, and the church more importantly. Ever since, I've been on a journey, asking the question, "Can we co-exist together?"

If you take your cues from cable news, you might give an emphatic "no" to that question. It sure seems like an impossibility, doesn't it? Conservatives want to be with conservatives, and progressives want to be with progressives. Is it simply that we have contrary opinions on social issues? Is it really just about policy differences? My hunch is that what's at work on me, on you, on all of us, touches something deeper than a piece of legislation or even who runs for president.

In my search for solutions to the polarization we are caught in, I discovered that Jesus, in the first century, faced the same emotional and spiritual gridlock we are facing. Jesus inhabited a boiling Crock-Pot of both progressives and conservatives (it's true, for real). It was thick and sticky and bitter. I wondered if there was a way, a peculiar way forward that Jesus carved out for this movement called Christianity. This was not a quaint exploration for me; the hostility we feel toward each other must be dismantled, or it will destroy us. It might be the most pressing issue of our time.

My exploration could not be a mental or merely abstract exercise—it had to be a full-bodied plunge. The more I pressed into polarization in my relationships, my neighborhood, and yes, on social media, something rattled my bones . . . FEAR. A full dose of fear of others: others I did not understand, others I disagreed with, others I had little in common with, others I honestly disliked. At every turn I wanted to take a step beyond polarization, fear was there to greet me and start erecting a fence. I had a fear problem, we have a fear problem, a serious one.

Fear is at the root of polarization, and it needs to be exca-
vated to make room for the growth of love, the unsurpassable
love of God. There is no comparison to the love displayed in
the life of Jesus. This love is most glorious, most brilliant, most
scandalous when it is poured out on those we are most frightened of. So this book is my journey of casting off fear to find
the way of love.

I made a few purposeful choices in how this book unfolds.
First, I wanted it to be personal, not addressed to the collective. The Church (with a big "C") certainly needs a collective wake-up call, but I wanted to start with the invitation to
my heart and your heart, a heart knowingly or unknowingly
controlled by fear. Second, I wanted this to be a book geared
to non-seminarians. The academy is grappling and bickering
about ideology, but I find much of it detached from the basic
feelings and fears I encounter on the ground, in my neighborhood, in my local relationships. I wanted to address the grass-
roots, the ordinary, those who'd never find a philosophy book
fun to read. Third, I wanted to integrate a cup of psychology, a
teaspoon of neurology, and a pinch of sociology, but at the end
of the day I wanted to fiercely focus on the real, revealed, rel-
evant life of Jesus. There are a thousand Scripture passages that
one could grapple with. Instead of bouncing around the Bible,
I wanted to keep us enraptured by the life of God in Christ.
The pathway forward is found in Him—so let's follow!

Chapter 1

THE WAY FEAR WORKS

Your relationship with fear is the most important one in your life because it's also a mirror of the relationship you have in your core. ◆ KRISTEN ULMER

It was hazy summer morning, grass damp from rainfall the day before. Dark was lingering as the sun was still creeping up, and I sauntered to the kitchen for my morning cup of coffee. Holding my favorite mug, I glanced out the window, and fear crashed upon me. My body shook as I saw what was outside. I dropped my mug, hot coffee splashing all around me, and I hit the floor and peered over the window sill. Twenty feet away, a man was pointing a gun at my house, and walking along my back fence. I didn't know what to do. Who wanted to kill us? I kept peeking over the sill, only to see him pacing back and forth, rifle aimed. I never felt such terror but found my bearings to crawl along the floor to find my phone to call 911. Suddenly my wife walked into the room. "Get down!" I yelled. She did, and I tried to explain the situation. She too looked over the sill; her response was not terror but confusion. "Dan, where is the gunman?" I pointed him out, but she still didn't see what I was seeing. "I see a squirrel scrambling along the top of our fence . . . is that your gunman?" Reality began to sink in. It was dark out, and I did not have my glasses on. I thought the outline of the squirrel and its bushy tale was a man holding a gun. I can laugh about this scenario now, and it makes for a great story to tell at parties, but I'm amazed how fear took over my senses. Just a little dim dawn, blurry eyes, and a groggy morning, and I believed I was the target of an assassination. I either have an inflated ego or need LASIK eye surgery. Fear dominated me so easily, so quickly. It has astounding strength to overpower our sense of sanity.

What do you fear?

There has not been a time in recent memory when our emotions, especially fear, have whipped us into a state of such alarm. If the recent election cycle is a mirror, then it's reflecting a society riddled with fear. It's not just threats of terrorism, economic collapse, cyber warfare, the police state, and government corruption; we fear each other, we fear strangers, we fear our neighbors, we fear those who vote differently, we even fear those who parent unlike us. We see each other primarily with the glasses of fear. Our current media outlets and professional politicians want to calcify your feelings on people, places, and things, convincing you to have an expert opinion on pretty much everything and everybody—even people you've never met. Just take a stroll down a Facebook feed to see everything our culture tells us to fear:

Alt-Right
Conservatives
Progressives
Feminists
White Supremacists
Immigrants
Muslims
Black Lives Matter
Evolutionists
Homeschoolers
Evangelicals
Pro-Lifers
The list goes on and on . . .

We see monsters everywhere right now, potential monsters hiding out in all kinds of places and behind the faces of all sorts of people. It all seems rational, it all seems logical, maybe even justifiable, but it is jet-fueled by the emotion of fear.

What is fear doing to us?

FEAR COMMERCIALIZED

After 9/11, fear built aggressive momentum in every aspect of American culture, especially in advertising. It takes sleight of hand to persuade a debt-saddled and ad-weary public that they should swipe their credit card for products. If you have no memory of being frightened into buying something, that's only because advertisers are magicians. Fear-based advertising is rampant, from off-road vehicles that never leave the streets to anti-aging cream that doesn't do anything. Marketing has long preyed on our insecurities and anxieties to sell us stuff that does not solve our problems but purposely pokes at our darkest fears that we don't have enough, don't know enough, aren't safe enough.[1]

Lately, hand sanitizers and antibacterial products have taken advantage of our pervasive fears of bacteria to market the notion that they can protect us from lethal diseases. One recent Purell ad positions the face of a cute puppy next to this quote: "Your best friend is actually your worst nightmare." Kellogg's also tried to jump on the disease-fearing bandwagon with a claim that their cereals bolster your child's immunity—the Federal Trade Commission debunked this claim and made them stop using it. The Food and Drug Administration has shown that the use of "antibacterial" products offers "no added health benefits," and now warns that they may cause harm.[2] And yet, the industry is booming.

Fear flat out works, which is why it is used in ads.

The oft-repeated phrase that "sex sells" turns out to be inaccurate after a little investigation. Sex just gets our attention. Fear sells units.[3] Why? The most likely reason: we want and need things to fear because fear is energizing. Not only has capitalism figured this out, but our entire political system has figured this out and turned it into well-honed strategies.

FEAR POLITICIZED

The raw experience of fearing a common enemy bands us together and can energize us to action. In the early 1980s, a group of psychologists developed a way to study how fear influences our behavior.[4] Their approach to understanding fear is using the Terror Management Theory. These psychologists were able to determine that, in general, when fear influences our decisions, we can be made to respond in wild ways. They assembled a long list of fear-based code words such as *hurt*, *danger*, *unsafe*, *peril*, *problematic*, *injure*, *sick*, *threat*, and then tested them out in various communication forums. These words elicited a dramatic response of action from people.

This language has become the constant drumbeat of American political speeches.[5] Politicians play to our gut fears of each other. Our leaders are now proficient in pulling our psychological strings to score a vote, but sadly, many of us are desensitized to it. Ironically, President Franklin Roosevelt said, "The only thing we have to fear is fear itself," yet here we are, and it's become the primary motivator in our times. Whether Republican or Democrat, young or old, we are easily romanced by the words of fear.

In contrast, when the language of hope, possibility, beauty, connection, and unity were used in the Terror Report, they flopped at stirring action. Positive language does not energize nearly as much as fear-based language does. Not surprising, this psychological Terror Management Report has become a formal guidebook for writing political speeches.[6] Both Republicans and Democrats use this report as a framework for peppering their speech with fear-based code words. Our political candidates have become masters of leveraging the psychology of fear.

Donald Trump delivered a speech that passionately used fear and threat: "The attacks on our police, and the terrorism in our cities, threaten our very way of life," Trump thundered. ". . . [Many] have seen the recent images of violence in our streets and the chaos in our communities. Many have witnessed this violence personally, some have even been its victims."[7]

Hillary Clinton wasn't any better, using the same tactic but for her preferred causes: "I'm the last thing standing between you and the apocalypse," she said.[8]

Fear is the language of our media powers. They understand

that to make their political interests become your political interests, they must trigger your moral gut. They must stimulate you to feel angry, or indignant, or threatened. This is their strategy to make you see monsters in the faces of other people.

FEAR WORKS WELL

Without fear, we feel unprotected by the world's dangers. In some situations, it is rational and reasonable to fear another person. For example, if someone physically threatens you, the best response is to run away screaming "stranger danger" as soon as possible. However, few of our interpersonal dealings involve such dire threats. Fear has its place, but it's like a forest fire in California when we welcome it unimpeded in our life.

Many of us cuddle and coddle fear because it just makes more sense than the generous, open posture of love. We believe love makes us vulnerable to harm while fear protects us. Love compels us toward people—fear creates a buffer. Love causes us to lean in and listen—fear tells us we don't need to hear any more. Fear offers something in return—a sense of control and safety, placing our wants, our needs, our anxieties at the center of importance.

> **Fear has its place, but it's like a forest fire in California when we welcome it unimpeded in our life.**

We sort of like fear. Fear gives us a strange kind of focus. At twelve years old, it was fear that coaxed me to take a different route to school so the neighborhood bully wouldn't see me and pick on me. Fear is a companion in some weird way. We feel deeply that if we don't stay on high alert, identifying what and who could hurt us, we are naive or even stupid. This is why fear resonates with the

American public more than love does. There is a concreteness and clarity to fear that comforts us—I know who to stay away from, I know who my enemies are, I know who to oppose, I know who to potentially hate.

WHAT MONSTERS FRIGHTEN YOU?

Maybe it's part of everyone's childhood, but I wish I could have skipped the stage where the monsters were under the bed. You know that part where you're up all night panicking that something is lingering underneath, waiting for you to fall asleep so it can gobble you up. I had many nights as a ten-year-old when I couldn't breathe. I'd have the covers pulled over my head, making sure my legs and arms were not too close to the edge. One night I had even devised a strategy for protecting myself. I set up my G.I. Joe action figures on the perimeter of my bed to keep guard because for some reason I was convinced the monster would not cross a toy soldier barricade. That was the first night in a while I fell asleep unafraid.

"Why are you so afraid?" Has anyone ever asked you this question? Have you ever asked it of yourself? You were probably asked some version of that question quite a bit when you were a little one as you faced the first day of going to school or jumping off the swing set at peak height or spending the night away from home for the first time. We know kids are afraid. We permit them to have fear. It's our job as adults to help nurture and coach them through this. But when you become a big person, it's viewed as weakness, cowardice, and humiliating to admit you're afraid. So we pose and pretend that we have no fear.

I'm no longer afraid of invisible monsters hiding under my bed, but I'm not sure you or I have rid ourselves of monsters

As adults, we outgrow specific fears, trade them in for new ones, and learn to mask them with a certain amount of sophistication.

that may not really be there. As adults, we outgrow specific fears, trade them in for new ones, and learn to mask them with a certain amount of sophistication.

Jesus grappled with this as He ministered and discipled people. They tried to hide behind their doctrines, spiritual clichés, and religious status, but Jesus had X-ray vision to see how constantly afraid they were. This is why Jesus asks of His disciples and the crowds, "Why are you so afraid?" almost forty times throughout the Gospels, and "Fear not" is the most frequently repeated command in Scripture—365 times! Three evenings after Jesus had been crucified and buried, the disciples are huddled in fear in an upper room with locked doors. Imagine the self-loathing and finger-pointing that filled the air: Whose idea was it to trust a guy from Nazareth? I can't believe I shut down my fishing business for this. Did Jesus trick us? My reputation is ruined. Who is going to get us something to eat up in here? Not me, I'm not going out there, we are a laughingstock. Now what?

When life is uncertain, when civilization seems unstable, fear is our first instinct. We huddle, we hunker down, we hide, we begin to hate the world. We seek the security of locked doors, gated communities, suspicious thoughts about others, talking through technology, impenetrable border walls, club memberships, and spending $500 billion annually on defense systems. I think Jesus knew something about us that we don't know about ourselves—we think and do a lot of stuff out of fear.

FEAR DISGUISED

Only a few years ago I convinced myself that one of my neighbors was a jerk—yup, that's what I thought, don't tell anyone. I walked past his driveway and out of the corner of my eye I saw him crawl out from under his car, sporting a red bandanna, slam a tool on the ground, and release an expletive. I thought, *Stay away from that dude.* I know I'm not the only one who has done this. I made a judgment from a distance about who he was. Somewhere in my mind, I allowed my perception to conveniently morph into a hard fact—HE IS A JERK. With no personal interaction and one snapshot of observation, I created a mental box that he was now stuck in. How does this happen so quickly? I confess now that my judgment of him was rooted in fear. He was unlike me. His hands were caked with grease, and I have little in common with motorheads (no offense). He symbolized something foreign to me, even intimidating to me from afar, and so I took a step back from connecting. Slowly, a man I never met was morphing into a perceived monster—someone I should be afraid of, and keep a distance. Fear impacts our spirit, our strength, our stamina to reach outward toward others unlike us. Fear ultimately affects love, silencing its voice in our lives.

I'M NOT AFRAID

What blocks most from addressing the fear in their lives? We don't think of ourselves as afraid. That word *fear* seems too blunt to us, unless we're talking about fear of snakes, spiders, or heights. When fear is not attached to concrete external objects, it's hard to identify. This is the nature of fear, to stay elusive, unable to be dealt with directly.

It reminds me of a conversation I had with a young husband who came to me for some counseling. His wife had asked him to meet with me because he was always on edge and barking out orders to his family. In our first session, I picked up some phrases that repeated in his speech. Two of them were the words *control* and *concerned*. These are typically code words for fear. So I asked him, "What do you fear?" He shot back an ironic response: "Fear? Fear is not an issue for me; I'm just afraid my family won't turn out the way it should!" He couldn't hear the confession in his statement. Even when I gently pointed out that he just said "afraid," the idea of "fear" was a step too far. Most of us don't recognize the signs of fear in our lives and therefore hold on to some level of self-delusion.

I have never viewed myself as a fear-based person either, but I've come to understand how fear is determined to put on disguises. It can be quite successful at masking its presence in our life. We can be pretty proficient at telling ourselves that fear has no part in our story. But we are mistaken. Fear wants to dress itself up, posing itself as "concern," so it has the power to place wedges between us and others.

When it came to encountering my blue-collar neighbor, my gut lurched ("he's probably a jerk"), and then I was not able to recognize a possible life-giving relationship with him. Fear disguised itself in my bloated opinion. A fearful person may even appear loving, but suspicion will interfere with the impulse to love someone unlike, different, or foreign—it depletes our energy for that action. When I felt the tinge of fear, rather than identifying it as such and exploring why, I tumbled into all kinds of mental gymnastics that allowed me, even entitled me, to label him. Fear is the enemy of love, and it will do whatever it can to disguise its face. Fear thrives in the shadows of our opinions, our rants, our judgments, and our preferred labels. Fear turns the face of the unfamiliar into perceived monsters.

DO I SEE MONSTERS?

We see this in the first disciples of Jesus. In Mark 9, Jesus sends out His little band of followers into the world to share the good news of His arrival, and then they discover someone unexpected. "Teacher," said John, "we saw someone driving out demons in your name and we told him to stop, because he was not one of us" (Mark 9:38). They are triggered by someone who is not like them, not one of them, not part of their tribe. They feel threatened, and a rogue demon-caster-outer becomes someone they fear. In the face of something foreign, their minds, their bodies, and their theology expelled rather than explored. They saw danger where there was none. Thankfully Jesus was there to correct their guttural response. "Do not stop him," Jesus said. "For no one who does a miracle in my name can in the next moment

In the face of something foreign, their minds, their bodies, and their theology expelled rather than explored.

say anything bad about me, for whoever is not against us is for us" (Mark 9:39–40).

Really? Does Jesus mean this? I can't imagine how this feels for the disciples. In their first-century world, there are so many lines and borders for who is in and who is out, who is good and who is bad, who is clean and who is dirty, who is acceptable and who is unacceptable. We have very similar

27

borders and lines that influence who we are afraid of, who appears dangerous to us. The disciples felt a fire within to oppose this fellow. He became someone they feared.

We turn people into monsters when we no longer see them as we see ourselves. Our status, enlightenment, education, race, theology becomes our comparative contrast against another. It makes us feel superior, although most of us would never publicly admit that. People don't have to do heinous evil things for us to see them as monsters; we just have to feel a tad better than they are. Something about their life feels offensive to us. Something about their politics or morals feels repulsive to us.

Ten years ago, I moved into the heart of Syracuse, New York, with my family. I'm embarrassed to admit it now, but I had to face a particular fear, diagnose it, and eventually dismantle it. One glorious spring afternoon, I was strolling through my neighborhood for the first time, taking in the sights and sounds. I squinted my eyes to see into the distance, and noticed a man was walking toward me on the sidewalk—a black man. I confess I felt a surge of fear move through my body. Maybe you're judging me as you read this. Often our fears don't hover on the tip of our tongue, they usually reside unprocessed, hiding out. The imprint of what frightens us doesn't "sit" in the verbal, understanding part of the brain. God is not scandalized, shocked, or disturbed by anything within us.

Was I afraid of black men? Could I openly acknowledge this? If you had asked me that question in conversation I would've absolutely said, "I have black friends." I'd push back, and might even be insulted by the question. Yet here I was, feeling fear, seeing a monster where there was none. It was all in my head. The temptation is to lie to ourselves, soothing our discomfort. Who wants to confess to being infected with racism? Delusion is more comfortable than daring to face the truth about ourselves.

Delusion is more comfortable than daring to face the truth about ourselves.

We all have latent fears of others when they're "not one of us," as the disciple John stated so matter-of-factly to Jesus. It causes us to avoid, dismiss, judge, and even hate others. The voice of fear speaks in very cut-and-dried terms; things are either good or evil, safe or dangerous, beautiful or ugly, right or wrong. Fear wants to be the ringleader of your emotions.[9] It wants to charge into the various rooms of our mind and yell "Fire!" Can we move beyond our initial reactions, automatic opinions, and perceived threats? The very soul of being a Jesus follower is at stake with how we answer this question.

FEAR INTERNALIZED

Sometimes I go all Superman with my son, put on a red blanket with its chew holes from our dog, and try to convince him that I am larger than life. Of course, no one is invincible. We are all fragile, easier to injure than we think, trying to make our way in the thickets of the universe. When we're young, we all lean toward idealism, assuming the best is inevitable, interpreting the world simplistically, good or bad.

Eventually we will collide with the immovable wall known as reality.[10] We become more alert to the harshness of the world as we accumulate nicks and cuts from the journey of life. Someone at some point steals from you, taking a measure of hope, a portion of joy, a feeling of peace. Someone you've loved moved away. Friends you've cared about stopped caring back. Leaders you've looked up to broke your trust. Someone you've let in close mistreated you. You have scars; I know I do. Fear is forged in the bowels of this hard world. So we look into the mirror and see our eyes; they are tired, showing the weight of cynicism. This is a necessary starting point, to look into a mirror honestly.

What has happened to me?
What has hurt me?

Honesty helps us breathe freely. Honesty is not bound to image-management and covering over the real.[11] Real honesty looks in the mirror. And this is precisely the kind of honesty that we need to face our fears.

What do we do when we realize we are not in control of the hurts that visit our lives? There is no erasing the experiences we live through. When we are injured, dashed, and royally let down, we begin to fear those around us—we look for monsters. When we lack control over the suffering in our lives, our fears direct us outward into suspicion rather than inward to confront the pain in our souls.[12]

I'd much rather grind against all that has damaged me— the slights that cut me, the ways people have taken advantage of me, the times I've been used up and tossed to the side. "Nobody deserves my love," says a bitter voice within. That voice wants to blast full volume in the echo chamber of my head. It wants to collect all the mistreatments, injuries, and betrayals, and assemble an airtight case that no one is worth loving. I feel the propulsion into the abyss, a closed and comfortable place of only loving myself and a few select people. Have you ever felt that shift within?

We close down, protecting what we have . . . we're afraid someone might ruin what good things we still have. Our souls feel divided though, don't they? We want to love generously, we wish to extend to others openly, but something pulls us back into the posture of self-protective fear.

How is fear shaping us?

As seen with my pathetic engagement with my neighbor, fear wants to flat-out

We want to love generously, we wish to extend to others openly, but something pulls us back into the posture of self-protective fear.

crush any compassion for anyone unlike me—my neighbor, the stranger, and my enemies. Our self-protective mechanisms kick in and create buffers between us. Honestly, I no longer felt a desire to discover who my bandanna-sporting neighbor was or who the black man was taking an afternoon walk. Fear ultimately does this—it shuts down relationships. This is quite arrogant, isn't it? We assume we know who someone is, and what they are about, from a snapshot, from a distance.

Acknowledging and naming my fears has opened me up to God, boldly inviting me to be changed by love, to live in love, and to be known by love (John 13:35). While we naturally loathe our enemies, Jesus showed us how to love them. We want to detest those who hurt us; Jesus taught us how to forgive them. We distance ourselves from those unlike us; Jesus showed us to share a meal with them. Jesus came to reveal and resolve a core problem—humanity's tendency toward fear. I needed to unpack how my inner fears were killing the expression of love.

Fear is not an abstract concept to be left to the sociologist to dissect intellectually; it is lurking in us all. Repressing fear in the chaos beneath can undoubtedly make you look put

We assume we know who someone is, and what they are about, from a snapshot, from a distance.

together, but you're not fooling anyone.

This is why the first words from an angel's mouth are often "fear not" when they encounter fragile, fumbling humans like us.[13] God understands we have reflexive fear in us. An angel tells the prophet Isaiah, "Do not fear . . ." (Isa. 41:10). In Matthew, an angel tells Joseph, "Do not be afraid . . ." (Matt. 1:20). In Luke, the angel tells Mary she's having a baby, and says, "Do not be afraid, Mary, for you have found favor with God" (Luke 1:30 NKJV). Then, when Jesus is born, an angel appears to shepherds watching their flocks and says, "Do not be afraid. I bring you good news . . ." (Luke 2:10). Fear is a significant blockage to seeing the God of love before us and around us. Fear shoves a potato sack over our head so that we cannot see. It limits our senses for feeling, knowing, and recognizing what love looks like in any given situation.

SCARCITY IS WHERE IT STARTS

Fear comes from a place of a tense, aching, insecure restlessness within us—a gurgling cauldron in the basement of our gut. Even though we may have virtually every practical reason to be happy—friends, health, material affluence—we experience an unsettled, insatiable, and disquieting discontent within.[14] The majority of us are dissatisfied. Research is showing that our mental and emotional state is at unprecedented lows. It's been traditionally thought that humans are generally pleased when they apprehend vocational goals, financial wealth, and good health, but neuroscientists are exposing that things "going well" doesn't make us happy. When a sampling of two thousand young people between the ages of twenty-five and thirty-five was tested multiple times throughout three years for feelings of well-being, they discovered a shocking reality. Even though their job satisfaction was high, their physical fitness was good, and their financial status was decent, their neurological receptors tested as agitated and unsatisfied.[15] What was discovered is that we have expectations that are not being met, but we are not sure exactly what those expectations are!

We have natural propensity to zone in on scarcity, to zero in on our lack. Scarcity is the emotional framework that "we do not have enough" of something: enough time, enough money, enough education, enough safety, enough energy, enough attention, enough strength, or enough to be okay. We believe we have too little, and the cost is that we feel "needy" instead of freehearted. I know this dwells in me, and it has shown up in how I'm tempted to parent my two-year-old son. There is a subtle but identifiable pull to buy the car seat built like a tank, to put gates on everything, to buy the crib with all the safety features, to buy the thermometer for bathtub time, to place a protective cover on the shopping cart, and even to buy the Owlet that sends oxygen stats to my phone while my baby sleeps. I have not fallen into that bottomless hole, but something inside says, "You're not doing enough to keep your baby boy safe." This is the voice of scarcity making me feel afraid.

"Scarcity promotes tunnel vision making us less insightful, less open, less safe, less free," writes Sendhil Mullainathan.[16] We seldom feel fully satisfied with our current status. We feel a few brief moments of euphoria, but we spend most of our lives waiting for a fuller amount to come.

Can you relate to this feeling? Are you waiting for something more to happen?

STINGY WITH LOVE

Many see the miracle in which Jesus divided the fish and loaves as a lesson on God fixing a problem of hunger; however, there is more to the scene. Five thousand people traveling a great distance and forgetting to bring food is highly unlikely. However, as time wore on, many people's supplies started to dwindle. Mom looks into the backpack and realizes there are no more snacks for the kiddos. I suppose that many in the crowd felt scarcity rather than generosity— stinginess settled in. Folks were less likely to share with those who had not prepared well for the day.

A young boy offers his loaves of bread and fish, and a miracle is sparked (Luke 9:10–17). Jesus is contradicting the everyday impressions that scarcity besets the world—that God's love and care are limited.[17] Jesus is confronting the fear that we don't have enough, that there is not enough to go around, that love is not enough.

Scarcity depletes our desire to be warm and welcoming to people who don't seem to have anything to offer us or who don't seem to have anything in common with us.

Jesus breaks in with a paradigm of plenty.

Jesus comes as the King whose kingdom flows with lavish love.

Jesus was guiding His disciples to live without fear in a world in which there seemed to be pervasive violence. When we feel like we don't have enough, we're stingy with who we're helpful to, who we're kind to, who we're openhearted to. When my heart is content and open, there is room to be present to anyone. When I am afraid, I turn in on myself and zone in on only those who are like me. Scarcity depletes our desire to be warm and welcoming to people who don't seem to have anything in common with us. When our lives are in a place of scarcity emotionally and mentally, we essentially hunker down into a state of self-preservation.

OUR SURVIVAL INSTINCT

Fear thrives off our powerful human instinct to survive. Our early ancestors were guided by the ability to survive, fight for their food, and continue to reproduce their own kind. Just about everything that humans have become has served that essential purpose. The way we relate with others illustrates our survival instincts. Fear is felt vigorously. This emotion signals an imminent threat to our well-being, which then triggers an urgent action in response to its cause (e.g., an attacker or rotten food).[18] This quick and forceful response keeps us alive and even prevents us from ingesting moldy broccoli that's been sitting in the back of the fridge for a month. Our senses are heightened when something frightens us or something repulses us, and so we make a judgment call. Without these instincts, our primitive forbearers would have died, and we wouldn't be chilling, perusing Pinterest, and sipping on Frappuccinos in the twenty-first century.

The most common threats to humans in primitive times remained relatively obvious—the danger from a wild animal or a rival tribesman. Maybe that's where we get "kill or be killed." Not much room for nuance in who is your enemy, right?

The notion of survival has changed dramatically in our first-world environment since the earliest days of humankind. I can't remember the last time I had to fight someone because they threatened my water source. Unlike threats of the past, today's threats are often in the form of ideas and opinions. Rather than moving toward each other, we obey our immediate survival-emotions. We react with fear because something about our life feels under attack, and we strike out verbally or virtually (gotta love social media). Fear rewires us for defense rather than discovery.[19]

OUR PRIMAL FEAR

We are wondrously made, and the more we discover this, the more we reveal how our bodies and brains are affected by fear. It has become increasingly verified through the developing science of neurology.

Nerd out with me a bit as I unpack this. We have three parts to our brain: the brain stem, the cerebellum, and the cerebrum. The first and smallest part of our brain is the stem. The stem controls breathing, heart rate, digestion, excretion, etc., which is why I short-circuit my brain stem the morning after I eat that late-night burrito.

The second and next most substantial part of our brain is the cerebellum. It is responsible for voluntary movements such as posture, balance, coordination, and speech, resulting in smooth and balanced muscular activity.

The third part of our brain is the cerebrum. For our exploration into fear there are two significant parts located here that are important to us. The amygdala, which is buried within the cerebrum and the prefrontal cortex, which is located at the outer layer of the cerebrum. The amygdala is responsible for emotions in human beings that are often impulsive or unconsciously automatic like disgust, laughter, fear, excitement, sex drive, and anger. Fear lights up the amygdala within this part of the brain. With many of these emotions that light up our brain, our bodies receive a robust chemical release of dopamine and serotonin. Fear is a primal response that does not require active contemplation, it is typically triggered when we feel threatened by another. We make our first judgments about what could hurt us quite rapidly, and we hardly ever seek evidence that might debunk our initial emotional judgment.

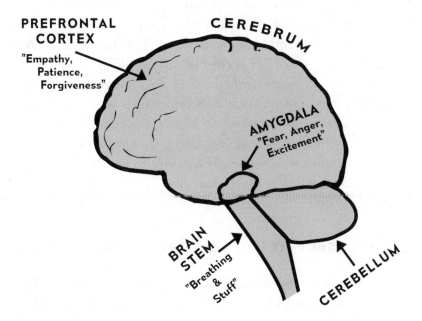

PREFRONTAL CORTEX
"Empathy, Patience, Forgiveness"

CEREBRUM

AMYGDALA "Fear, Anger, Excitement"

BRAIN STEM "Breathing & Stuff"

CEREBELLUM

The prefrontal cortex is associated with higher, more complex brain functioning such as empathy, forgiveness, self-control, patience, hospitality, and listening (not just hearing), etc. Though the prefrontal cortex is the largest part of our brain, it is the least utilized part by the majority of the population. Dr. Joshua Greene said "our best estimates are that only 10% of the population uses their prefrontal cortex on a regular basis. Theoretically, it's possible to go your whole life and never use this part of our brain."[20] Why is this? The prefrontal cortex requires the development of higher thinking while the amygdala is essential but impulsive and in many ways lower thinking.

It takes mindful, careful work to move beyond the automatic impulse of fear. Because the amygdala is the source of fear, it produces a dose of dopamine and serotonin as a reward in our bodies. Think about that—fear gives us a dose of drugs, a feel-good chemical. As counterintuitive as it sounds, fear feels good. When someone makes a fear-based statement about another, I like to say, "That's just the drugs talking."

In contrast, the prefrontal cortex does not generate those type of potent chemicals and therefore feels less rewarding. No wonder we are hooked on fear; we've become junkies. Fear is as primal as primal gets. Being afraid of others—who could hurt us or who are simply repelling to us—is quite natural, but Jesus followers are being called out of the natural into something unusual, supernatural even.

SECURITY TO SELF-PROTECTION

All of this fear can be traced back to humanity's origins. The story starts with a God who profoundly enjoys making the world. The Father, the Son, and the Spirit engage in a fascinating conversation about how to make humanity: "'Let us make mankind in our image, in our likeness, so that they may rule over the fish in the sea and the birds in the sky, over the livestock and all the wild animals, and over all the creatures that move along the ground.' . . . God blessed them and said to them, 'Be fruitful and increase in number; fill the earth and subdue it.' . . . Then God said, "I give you every seed-bearing plant on the face of the whole earth and every tree that has fruit with seed in it. They will be yours for food. . . . God saw all that he had made, and it was very good" (Gen. 1:26, 28–29, 31). It's as if God builds a gorgeous home and manicures a ridiculously beautiful yard and tells the first humans, "Look what I made for you . . . for realz!" (paraphrase mine).

God creates out of community of Father, Son, and Spirit as the fountain of love brimmed over. They enjoy one another, and They enjoy us! That is why God uses the term "very good" to describe the situation. God is providing for and caring for Adam and Eve, and it's very, very good. The first words about us are that we have received the good life. And it's all holy, it's all sacred. The whole world is God-bathed. It's drenched in love.

Let's not miss that the Trinity is not saying everything is perfect. In fact, in Genesis 2:18, God describes Adam's alone state as "not good," and that is before things go sour and sin enters into the world. It's important to understand that the main point of the garden of Eden is not that it's a place of perfection, but that it's a place of presence—God's abiding presence.

Adam and Eve are not on their own to look out for themselves. This is good news for you, for me, and for the world around us. Our lives do not have to be perfectly manicured. Our lives do not have to be perfectly hemmed in with safety barricades. Our wants don't have to perfectly provided for. God is with us in the midst of our ordinariness. God is present in our imperfect lives, and this changes everything.

Then the voice of fear slithers its way into the love-soaked garden of Eden and plays with our head. The Bible reveals this voice to be Satan (2 Cor. 11:3), the tempter (1 Thess. 3:5), the one who comes to steal, kill, and destroy (John 10:10). The serpent introduces the first rustlings of fear, pretending to be our ally. Fear begins to pick at us: "Are you sure you have enough? Are you really secure? Isn't someone holding out on you?" It points fingers, blames others, and talks into our soul, masquerading as "wisdom."[21] It's quite interesting that Satan is called "more crafty than any of the wild animals the LORD God had made" (Gen. 3:1). This is one of the ways fear disguises itself: "Well, I'm just being wise." This is not the voice of divine love; it's the voice of self-protective fear.

Fear tells us love is not enough: "Maybe I'm not okay, maybe I don't have enough, maybe I'm not safe," shifting us into a self-preserving state. This is why Adam and Eve run, hide, and start a new fashion trend of wearing fig leaves. They are convinced they must protect themselves, cover themselves, and separate themselves to be safe. Where there was once harmony, there is now hostility. Ever since, all of humanity has been haunted by apparitions that if we don't first take care of ourselves and our interests, then no one will. This turn toward self-protection is a sad theme throughout the Scriptures.

Being alive is a scary, unpredictable experience, but Jesus is inviting us into a different way of being in the face of the unfamiliar, in the face of our perceived monsters. Jesus is calling us out of our survival instincts, out of our politics of fear, out of our perceptions of others, into a lush landscape of love. We sense it, we feel it beneath our feet, but we look up and see it overhead—fear and love are at war.

Reflection Questions

1. What is the big idea that sticks out to you in this chapter?

2. What part of "how fear works" brings you some conflict or clarity in your life?

3. What practical step can you take to unplug from the culture of fear in and around your life?

Chapter 2

LOVE AND FEAR AT WAR

Once a person learns to read the signs of love and thus to believe it, love leads him into the open field wherein he himself can love. ◆ HANS URS VON BALTHASAR

I've never been a great sleeper—toss, turn, rub my tense legs, wander down the stairs for a drink of water. The night triggers my body to amp up for tomorrow's challenges. It takes the stars to align for me to rest through the night. I hear every sound at 2:00 a.m., but on one October night, I heard monsters. They were outside my window. I was already up, so I split apart our curtains to take a peek. Under the haze and the flickering streetlight, I could see three men dragging another man down the sidewalk. Was this a game of some sort? They stopped in front of my house, picked him up, and walked up to my driveway with purpose. I found out later that they had already shot him in the arm about a block away. They lifted him and sprawled him out on the hood of my car. The sounds of his groans still echo in my memory. I watched every cruel, rage-filled blow from their baseball bats as they bludgeoned this young man into oblivion.

Our neighborhood galvanized to organize against the constant gang violence. But I privately could not shake the images of hell from my mind. Night terrors of wickedness became a regular occurrence. The morning after the violent event I rinsed off the dried blood covering my car. As I washed away what remained, I felt deep fear in my chest. What if those three men are watching me now? I'm the one who called 911 on them. Could I get over my fear? The fear began to take over. I made plans to move out of the neighborhood God had called my wife and me to.

THE ESSENCE OF GOD

In 1 John 4:18 we encounter this potent passage: "There is no fear in love. But perfect love drives out fear, because fear has to do with punishment. The one who fears is not made perfect in love." If you're a Star Wars geek, then this passage might remind you of something Yoda once said: "Fear is the path to the dark side. Fear leads to anger. Anger leads to hate. Hate leads to suffering."[1] Fear is the source of all kinds of destruction.

Those words "perfect love casts out fear" were written in the context of a conflict that caused a split in a community. The apostle John is laying out the war—Love and Fear are opposed to each other. They cannot coexist. They are like oil and water, fire and ice, deep-fried Oreos and Weight Watchers—they are opposites.

Some of our fears are legitimate and others illegitimate,

but we feel them fiercely either way. I feared for my family. I felt anxiety on the sidewalks that I once peacefully strolled through my neighborhood. Our worries rise up daily, but the Spirit is calling us to rise above our survival instincts and put on the new clothes of love offered to us in Jesus. After that violent scene on my front lawn, my amygdala was screaming for me to move out, to be with people more like myself. I'd be safer living with people who share my values. Fear wanted to imprison my decisions, but only love could bring me freedom. Only love has the power to win the war against fear.

This probably sounds too flimsy as a real plan of action. Maybe your response to "love" being the solution is, "Oh, that's all? Just love?" Love seems soft. Sentimental. Sappy. Something you graduate from and then move on to more substantial things.

Really, Is Love Strong Enough?

When we look at what the New Testament has to say about love, it's shocking how powerfully it is portrayed. At the end of the day, you've got "faith, hope and love. But the greatest of these is love" (1 Cor. 13:13). The apostle Paul is explicit: we have nothing, absolutely zilch if we do not have love. But what does this mean to us? For the most part, many Christians have a weak imagination for love. The word "love" has collapsed into greeting card well-wishes, trendy justice hashtags, romantic comedies, and spiritual clichés that appear in our modern worship songs.

This remarkable insight that "perfect love casts out fear" is located earlier in 1 John's bold confession that God is love: "Whoever does not love does not know God, because God is love" (1 John 4:8). We cannot know God more without increasing our capacity for love. Love is the means and the end.

The very essence, the very being of God is love itself. God IS love. We wake up some days and feel more generous toward people, and other days we wake up like a Mack truck hit us and feel cranky. Love is not merely one of God's many moods. God is love, always love.

Before anything existed in the universe, there was love. Before any creature crawled on the ground or any bird glided through the air, there was the river of God's love flowing. It is the first reality. In John 17:24, Jesus shares a glimpse of this pre-world existence. As Jesus is talking to the Father, He says, "You loved me before the creation of the world." Love starts with the Trinity—the Father, the Son, and the Spirit. What bonded Them together was not obedience, or a hierarchy, or any other attribute. Love is the relational mortar; They have been self-giving in Their love before human time ever existed.[2] This flowing river of God's love stands as a contrast to our raging tsunami of fear. This truth is foundational.

Usually when we describe someone, we describe them with adjectives or nouns. Like, "Oh Dan is an awkward (adjective), portly (adjective) fellow (noun)." How do we describe God? If you picture the world as a house, standing strong and sturdy, the base of it, the bottom row of rocks that holds everything else up—GOD IS LOVE. The very essence of God *is* love. When we reach for words, this is our best description of God from our limited vantage point. God is love. It has always been this way and always will be. But to say the character of God *is* love is not enough, right? Action must flow from character to confirm it is real. It would be like saying "Dan is an awkward guy" but not having any awkward actions to observe (I guarantee you there are plenty of those to observe). The love (noun) of Father, Son, and Spirit becomes an action (verb) occurring in the universe. The character of God's love materializes as action, love happening to us and around us and through us, always, without ceasing.

We are in God's world, where all that exists is being touched and transformed by the divine hands of love. God's overflowing, bounteous love is holding the very seams of our universe together, or else it would fall apart. We are children of God, born out of the Father, the Son, and the Spirit's circle of unending love.[3] We are love's offspring. This is the closest we can get to describing God adequately with words.

IS GOD LOVE?

This is the nagging question under the surface of humanity and every human heart: "Is God love?" There is insecurity in our answers. As children floating through the sea of existence, detached from God's undeniable, physical presence, we are unsure. I can't tell you how many times, in my most painful seasons, I craved to lean over and cry on God's shoulder. Prayer is beautiful, the Scriptures are meaningful, but nothing replaces real-time proximity. This is why our bodies groan, and our spirits cry out for the kingdom come. The fullness of God's presence is not yet here. So in the meantime, questions linger . . . is God really love?

I was scared of a lot of things as a kid—sitting on a wasp, the clown from the '90s TV movie *It*, the SAT, taking my shirt off to go swimming, having no one to sit with during lunch in the cafeteria, faulty parking brakes—but nothing scared me more than God. God, in my mind, was like the vacuum cleaner salesman who gushes with goodwill until you decide not to buy a vacuum cleaner. The moment I sinned, God was ticked off at me. God could see all my thoughts, a faceless deity interrogated my every action, waiting to punish me when I didn't follow the rules. As a teenager, when I said I loved God, I meant I depended on being on His good side. I understood reward and punishment and fear. If I did bad things, God would spank me. If I did good things, God would bless me. I didn't genuinely know what affection for God felt like, let alone what God's affection for me felt like. Somewhere in my belly, the fear of God was far more emotionally palatable than the love of God. It seems evident to me now that to have a caring, enjoyable relationship is difficult when one party is threatening to hurt you if you don't love them back.

LOOKING PAST GOD

We often have a picture of God floating around in our mind's eye that we don't usually give words to. This God stirs up emotion, reaction, and passion in us. When most think of God, they filter out anything that is not superhuman, supersized, and larger than life. Just forming the word "God" with our lips conjures up a Zeus-looking character who is sitting high above the earth on Mount Olympus, sending down lightning bolts of punishment on the world.[4] In the imagination of those who do believe and don't believe in God, I consistently find similar portrayals. God is supposed to present Himself in big ways. That's what gods do, right?

Two thousand years ago, the Israelites had volumes of material on God (Yahweh) and were convinced He would present Himself in a "big" way. This would only make sense to them since their interpretation of the Law led them to look for a certain type of God. This God would eventually destroy their enemies and elevate them to glory. Jesus understood that these misinterpretations were floating around.

You can understand why John the Baptist is a tad confused

48

at the appearance of Jesus when he asks, "Are you the one who is to come, or should we expect someone else?" (Luke 7:19). John is looking for an Elijah figure.[5] "Surely the day is coming; it will burn like a furnace. All the arrogant and every evildoer will be stubble, and the day that is coming will set them on fire. . . . I will send the prophet Elijah to you before that great and dreadful day" (Mal. 4:1, 5). According to these prophetic words, violent justice against pagan Gentiles will be the shining sign that the Messiah has arrived. John the Baptist is looking for this clear expression. What is John the Baptist's fear? That God may not burn up the wicked, that evil will prevail, that the righteous will not make it out on top. No wonder he's thrown off by this compassionate Christ.

Curiously, the Romans who did not believe in Yahweh believed God would present Himself in a similar "big" way. When God was dying on a wooden cross, they mocked Him for claiming to be God, saying, "Call your angels and bring yourself down if you're God" (paraphrase Matt. 27:40). They had expectations that a god would look a certain way, and Jesus sure did not look like any god they were familiar with. Even Greek culture knew how kings were supposed to claim their victory over enemy opposition. When we look at Jesus, we are presented with a God that does not look like a god according to our standards, wants, or expectations.

It seems even the disciples who get close to God have a hard time recognizing God. Philip said, "Lord, show us the Father and that will be enough for us." I can imagine Jesus rolling His eyes and rubbing His head like I do when my kids say, "Is this all we got for Christmas?" Jesus answers: "Don't you know me, Philip, even after I have been among you such a long time? Anyone who has seen me has seen the Father. How can you say, 'Show us the Father'?" (John 14:9). It's easy to miss God when we are looking for something particular.

This reminds me of when I'm looking for a lost piece of mail. Ripping my desk apart, I pick through everything, and I still can't find it. My wife meanders over, sees it in a couple of seconds, and plops it onto my lap. I look at it realizing I couldn't find it because in a frenzy I was looking for the envelope with the red logo on it, not the blue one. I narrowed my search so much that I was only looking for what was already pictured in my mind.

We miss God because we are looking for something specific, according to our expectations. Up to this point, the primary way in which God manifested was in a cloud (Ex. 16:10) or in a tablet of stone (Ex. 34:1). When Jesus appears, everyone looked past Him—they were looking for something else, and we still do. We expect God to look a certain way. The Bible does not give us an abstract definition of "God is love"—it ultimately provides us with the person of Jesus.[6] We value our one-sentence definitions, but God cannot be contained in Webster's dictionary—Jesus is our definition of love with flesh on it. Only the undiluted Jesus defines God. He is the image of the invisible (Col. 1:15).

To this day, Christianity is still struggling with this. We are still reaching for ways to explain and define God without beholding the life of Jesus.

Jesus is what the Old Testament was trying to say but never fully articulated.[7] It can't be any more evident that God didn't say all that needed to be said in the form of a book or Ten Commandments, so He said it in the form of the person Jesus. We can pick and choose verses from the Bible to construct a Zeus-Looking God. Many have been taught this is what it means to be faithful to the Bible. But to be faithful to the Bible is to accept the terms the Bible gives us—every other portrait of God is subordinate to Jesus Christ. This is a bold claim. The glorious truth of God's character is fully articulated in Jesus, who is the true and living Word of God. Jesus is the ultimate and complete self-manifestation of God (John 1:14). This changes everything about how we imagine God.

Does this mean God inspired the Old Testament? Of course, it does. The role of the Old Testament is important; it tells us the twisty drama of how we get to Jesus and why we need Jesus. You cannot cut Jesus off from the narrative of the Old Testament, but you must understand that the revelation of God in the Old Testament bows down to the revelation of God, in the flesh, in Jesus. Some might want to pitch the Old Testament, feeling it's too primitive, and others want to read the Bible like a flat text where every passage carries the same weight. Neither will do. Jesus is the pair of bifocals we put on to read and understand all of Scripture. Jesus is the picture of God, the prototype for living, and the pathway for healing the world. Over the years, the more I've mediated on the glorious revealing of God in the person of Jesus, the more my fear has fallen away, and the more love has sprouted in its place.

The more I've meditated on the glorious revealing of God in the person of Jesus, the more my fear has fallen away, and the more love has sprouted in its place.

God comes to us as wholly other—unlike the gods we imagine.[8] The full-bodied life of Jesus is helping us imagine God differently. We cannot piece together a few verses here and few verses there to get our images of God.[9] We find our definitions and contours of love by looking, no, staring at Jesus. If we do not, we will miss God, and tragically miss love.

IT'S NOT ALL ABOUT WORDS

What makes love, and ultimately God, challenging to define is that it has less to do with the words we say ("telling"). I get the question all the time: "What does the Bible say?" Often we are looking for a backup for our actions by finding words in the Bible to support them. Certainly, words have something to do with following Jesus, but it goes far beyond them.

We have all probably observed this when we have asked someone if they are upset with us and they respond, "No, everything is fine." But their body language is communicating the exact opposite. Our bodies can betray our words. Words are meaningful, but they can somehow sit on the surface like leaves lying on the top of a swimming pool. You see them, but they cover up what's fermenting underneath. I've run into far too many Christians who know the words of the Bible, memorized a slew of verses, and can quote them to prove their point, but underneath, below the surface, they are grumpy, judgmental, prideful, bitter, and impatient with others. Words are not enough—they're good, but there is something deeper, more profound.

IT'S NOT ALL ABOUT WHAT

Dare I say it's not about the "what" either. I hate to confess that my wife has asked me to do something for her, and I've done it, but I've stomped around like a bratty child, huffed and puffed but got the job done. Afterwards, she's gently stated, "I'd rather you not do it if you're going to do it with an attitude." Ouch! So true. There is something more, something mysterious that matters to us, isn't there?

I'm reminded of this in church history where the "what" betrayed what was going on under the surface. Roman politics in AD 305 was confusingly complicated as emperors of the West and the East contended for power. Among them was Flavius Valerius Constantinus, known to history as Constantine the Great. He won a significant battle in AD 324, which made him master of the entire Roman Empire, but he is most famous for his conversion to Christianity, which would prove to be a cataclysmic event.[10] Constantine was a pagan monotheist before his conversion. In his zealousness and understanding of God's revelation, he battled with the Christian symbol of the cross marked on his soldiers' shields. He had overwhelming victories, slaughtering thousands of enemies, and he attributed it to the Christian God.[11] The sign of the cross marked his rule and reign. Constantine as a Christian vigorously promoted Christianity and propagated it by use of raw force. Constantine and his army would worship "what" Christ did on the cross, and then on Monday go out and kill pagans. Constantine perpetuated a Zeus-Looking God. It's quite possible to sing worship songs about what Jesus did and miss the way of Jesus entirely. It's not just the "words" or even the "what" that reveals who we are.

I think this is what the apostle Paul was getting at in 1 Corinthians 13:1–3:

> If I speak in the tongues of men or of angels, but do not have love, I am only a resounding gong or a clanging cymbal. If I have the gift of prophecy and can fathom all mysteries and all knowledge, and if I have a faith that can move mountains, but do not have love, I am

nothing. If I give all I possess to the poor and give over my body to hardship that I may boast, but do not have love, I gain nothing.

What we do and what we say can be meaningless. Paul says they equate to nothing, nada, zip! A modern parallel is we can lead a dynamic worship event or have an extensive grasp of biblical knowledge or be a passionate social justice warrior, but without the way of love, it is nothing. It is easy to trick ourselves and others that we are loving, but it can all be smoke and mirrors. We need love, but it must burrow below the surface.

IT'S ABOUT THE WAY

We all want to say the right things (words) or do the right things (what), but we need an awakening to the *way* of perfect love. God is not a being who decides to love occasionally, but God is the one in whom "we live and move and have our being" (Acts 17:28). This is not just a religious statement; it is also a deeply metaphysical one.

What do I mean by metaphysical? No, I'm not getting all New Age on you. We are surrounded by metaphysical forces all day. Gravity is a metaphysical force, a force that is unseen, transcendent, but practically pulls us downward, keeping our feet planted on the ground. Love is a metaphysical force as well, and might be the most important one. Love is a state that includes what we do and words we say but goes far beyond them to a way of being—a transcendent truth but perceivable by our senses.[12] Perfect love is an external reality that we resist or submit to. Gravity pulls us downward. Love ultimately pulls us outward, toward others, toward the stranger, the widow, the foreigner, the poor, and most shockingly, toward our enemies. This love is the Spirit of Jesus in us, around us, available to us, which is why we are invited to "[live] in love" (1 John 4:16). We are evoked to listen to the current of love, in Jesus who is God. As stated earlier, this love already existed before the

We treat Jesus merely like an event to celebrate rather than a daily path to walk.

foundation of the world. It is higher than you and me but invites and includes you and me.

This way of perfect love was fleshed-out in Jesus. We treat Jesus merely like an event to celebrate rather than a daily path to walk. Jesus embodies this metaphysical force in His lived life.

This metaphysical force, is perfect love. We can sense it, but we regularly let fear overtake it. Jesus lived, as fully human, in conscious connection to the love of God. It empowered Him to say yes to perfect love that casts out fear.

CASTING OUT FEAR

When you're looking to figure out what love looks like, don't look at celebrity preachers on stages, or politicians using religious slogans in speeches, or even your parents who took you to Sunday school classes—they will disappoint. They cannot carry the weight of the revelation of God's love. We must unpack the profundity that God the Father sent Jesus the Son in the power of the Spirit to explain, example, and expose the abounding love of the triune God. Look, listen, and let go to this current.

Our transformation as beautiful and broken people has everything to do with tuning the dials of our eyes and ears to the way of love versus the way of fear. The language is so bright and direct that the power of this contrast can easily be lost on us. Let it sink in for a moment. If God *is* love, and perfect love casts out fear, then fear is the *opposite* of everything that God *is*.

SHOULD WE FEAR GOD?

What about the often-repeated phrase in the Bible "the fear of LORD"? Maybe you've been raised to "Fear God," but this makes it really difficult to genuinely warm up to God. This terrifying fear might come to mind for you. The Scriptures illustrate a wrong kind of fear.[13] A specific one is the parable of the servants: the unprofitable servant was corrected for being lazy after he made an excuse, "I was afraid, and went and hid your talent in the ground" instead of using it productively (Matt. 25:25 NKJV). Such fear does not have a positive and productive end. Obviously, this fear is not what God is looking for.

When the Bible says, "Fear God," the Hebrew verb *yare*, which is often translated fear, means "to respect, to revere" and is often associated with believing God's good intentions (Ex. 20:20) or making a person receptive to wisdom (Prov. 1:7; 9:10). The Greek noun *phobos* also means a "reverential attitude" of God. I honestly think that the word "fear" is an ill-suited English translation from those Hebrew and Greek words.

We confuse fear and reverence. We are to revere God, to believe that God's presence, and all-consuming love, is all we need to be satisfied in life. Brennan Manning said it well: "The sorrow of God lies in our fear of Him."[14] In the garden of Eden, the Enemy called into question Adam's and Eve's reverence for God—that God was over all and through all, that God was the supreme source for that which was good in life. It's like trying to make it as a musician, having multiple Grammy award–winning artist Elton John as a next-door neighbor but scoffing at seeking out his counsel and feedback. To revere someone's authority on a subject compels us to seek their wise input and instruction. This is a better imagination for understanding the word "fear" in relation to God. We are not commanded to fear God in the medieval sense that someone might torture us, or even in the popular sense that someone might beat us up. The language of "the fear of the LORD" is intended to convey a positive reverence, the desire to seek God as the source for the good life.

Certainly, the pendulum can swing in the opposite direction. Some fear the reverence of God. God's authority seems off-putting, stifling, even offensive. When the primary image of God in society has been one we should fear because He holds malice over our heads, the overreaction is to piece together an image of God that looks like the opposite. I call this the Self-Esteem God. This God has little authority to place constraints on our choices or costly commands on our life. Authority is shifted to the inner self. The Self-esteem God puts our insecure and unsatisfied ego at the center of our world, not the authority of Jesus. We manufacture a god that becomes primarily concerned with the maintenance of our own wants and wishes, zeroed in on making sure we have good vibes about ourselves. But we all know intuitively the "self" is never satisfied; it is black hole that will seek to absorb all the energy of relationships for personal consumption or soothing affirmation. In this pendulum swing, we become god and the real God orbits around us. My hunch is that there are small slivers of truth in both the Zeus-Looking God and even the counter-reaction of the Self-Esteem God. Yet neither of these capture the revelation of God that looks like Jesus.

Our image of God often falls far short of God's unsurpassable love portrayed in the words, works, and ways of Jesus. Is this your imagination for God? Do you see the Zeus-Looking God or the Self-Esteem God? Or do you see Jesus?

The situation is epic, but the implications are exceptionally personal. Our fear must be faced, renounced, and dismantled because it seeks to steal, kill, and destroy the way of love. It is ravaging the soul of Christianity. If perfect love casts out fear, then perfect fear will seek to cast out love. To put it more starkly, fear casts the God revealed in Jesus out of our lives and churches. The way of fear is the broad path, the most open highway. We fear our enemies, we fear God, we fear everything. My fear of my biker-neighbor reached up, wrapped its hands around my heart, and squeezed tight to choke out any movement of love toward him. We need to begin to grasp how deep and hidden the problem is.

At the nexus of the universe, at the crux of each heart, is a war between Love and Fear. Your whole life and the entirety of Christianity is bound up in this war. To summarize Christian philosopher Søren Kierkegaard, "Since the early goings of the Genesis story, fear became the core illness in the human condition. It is no mistake that Scripture repeats the words, 'Do not fear' and 'Do not be afraid' over and over. It is the central emotion in opposition to the work of love."[15]

At the nexus of the universe, at the crux of each heart, is a war between Love and Fear.

As a follower of Jesus, to act in fear toward others is antithetical to the character of God, for God is love. Fear seeks to control the story of our life as we exhaust mental bandwidth, make panicked choices, and form reactive opinions about others. God is always and relentlessly drawing us into love. Fear wants to be our constant companion.

REDEFINING PERFECTION

We need a movement of love. As our culture is locked in a war between the conservative right that wants the power to legislate morality (among other things) and the progressive left that wants the power to legislate social justice (among other things), we need another way. There is a fear hiding deep within us all that wants to command and control all our interactions. We are being called out of this way of engaging the world, our families, our friends on social media. We are being boldly invited as those formed in love, by a God of love, to be perfect in our love.

What does "perfect" mean? Can we really be perfect?

First John says that "perfect love casts out fear." This same descriptor of love is used in Matthew 5 when Jesus tells His disciples to "be perfect, therefore, as your heavenly Father is perfect." The word "perfect" that we effortlessly use so much is often misunderstood. We tend to apply an unqualified Webster's dictionary meaning to it ("without error") or put it into an unachievable category. Then Jesus' command to "be perfect" is merely a laudable goal, one that is impossible for human beings. It is easy to quote this line and be overwhelmed by its moral flawlessness. The problem in this line of thought is that the Hebrew word (*tamim*) does not carry the same meaning of "without error" in an absolute sense as does the term "perfect" in English.[16] *Tamim* means complete or whole. So let's try replacing "perfect" with the word "whole" for a minute. Say it like this: "*whole* love casts out fear" or "be whole as your Father God is whole." The whole of something implies that it's not just a part of something, not only a portion, or a slice.

IMAGE-BEARER OR MONSTER

Our understandings and practices of love are very thin, *not* whole. We want to love people like us, the people who vote like us, the people who think like us, the people who believe like us. We embrace a partial love, not a perfect love. Only a whole love can turn our perceived monsters into possible friends. Why? Because there is nobody, no matter how damaged or damaging, who does not carry the image of God—a wholehearted love does not close down to this reality.

This word *image* has its roots in the creation story in Genesis. The Father, Son, and Spirit making a bunch of stuff. All kinds of stuff like water and earth and stars and kangaroos and even the most annoying creation of all . . . mosquitoes. But God is just warming up. God places something unlike any other creation into the mix—human beings. "Let us make human beings in our image" (Gen. 1:26 MSG). When we read this part, what lifts to the surface is that everything else prior was not given this status "in our image." We can debate what the Genesis creation account is about. Is it about gender roles, is it about six literal days of creation, is it about environmentalism? Those are all interesting discussions, but what is spotlighted in the text is that God places His *image* into this aspect of creation. The simple truth that is that people are the crown jewel of God's creative work.

To fully latch onto the depths of what is being established in the cosmos, we must dive deeper into the language used. The Hebrew word for image is *tselem* [teseh'elem], which means a physical replica of something.[17] Generally, *tselem* is used to refer to something representing the image of a deity. When you see a statue of Alexander the Great, you assume it "looks like" Alexander the Great. The image reminds you of the original because it's patterned after the original. Are there

60

variations? Of course, no statue is an exact replica. This is a huge deal established in the biblical narrative—we, me, you, all humans hold the image of God, the Supreme Being that started and holds this whole crazy world together.

But the question lingers: Is it possible that sin can destroy the image of God so much that it no longer exists? While the fall in Genesis has stripped away our ability to keep God's ideals for us, it did not rob us of God's image.[18] Despite our own brokenness and proneness to wander from living in the love of God, we have a deeper goodness that cannot be obliterated. Our actions may not look like God, but our very essence holds the *tselem*. This is the deeper truth we look for, we search for, we gain eyes for in others. Beyond the surface of behaviors, we look for God in the soul of another. Is it harder to see in some more than others? Of course. But not only did Jesus come to show us what God looks like, He also came to show us how to look at people. Since humanity is created in the image of God, a human being is a microcosm of the divine.

Not only did Jesus come to show us what God looks like, He also came to show us how to look at people.

GOD IN OUR IMAGE

Sadly, we often reverse things, and instead of understanding that we are made in the image of God, we imagine God in our image. As did many of the characters in the Bible, we look for a god who fears what we fear, who hates what we hate, who likes what we like, who affirms what we affirm. God operates in a manner so often unlike what we are ready to receive that we craft a god that is merely a projection of our human desires.

We are all tempted to finagle God to fit our fears and engage the world as we do. Many conservatives have fashioned a god that looks like a red-state, Ten-Commandments-monument-advocating, strict-Constitution-defending politician, and many progressives have fashioned a god that looks like a blue-state, sexual-freedom-advocating, free-health-care-protecting politician. One group sees Jesus protesting in front of an abortion clinic and another group sees Jesus protesting with Black Lives Matter. We all want to baptize God into our *tselem* fully—"in the name of myself, my opinions, and hobby horses, amen."

We look for a god who fears what we fear, who hates what we hate, who likes what we like, who affirms what we affirm.

Our world is swinging between the caricatures of a conservative-looking God and a progressive-looking God. Behind many of our agendas are fear, not love. We tend to place a mirror between God and us so that we see ourselves and our agendas. We begin to think God's love is just as narrow as our love is. We are all made in the *tselem* of God, not the other way around. We turn people into monsters to fear when we get this all mixed up.

LOVING THE WHOLE

We must love the whole indiscriminately. As a follower of Jesus, we should not assess the compatibility we have with others and whether they will become an object of our love. God's love is indiscriminate, loving the whole. This is perfect love. Love that is not selective, not choosy, not zeroed in on people we think we have something in common with. Many of us say we love everyone, but practically we are partial in our love. We pick and choose who will receive our kindness, our compassion, our warmth, our presence.

Here are a few questions to consider: Who do we mean when we say God loves us? Who is us? When did we allow the word "us" to become so small? What people are not inside your "us"?

We must move beyond sentimentality and into reflection. This has been a helpful practice for me in being honest about who it is it hard for me to see the image of God in. Who do I like to keep a distance from? Who do I see as my enemy politically? Or theologically?

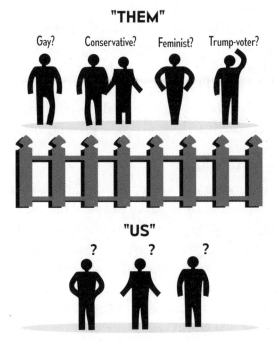

Can you see the image of God in abortion doctors?

Can you see the image of God in the LGBTQ community?

Can you see the image of God in your ultraconservative grandpa?

Can you see the image of God in your political enemies?

Can you see the image of God in rednecks?

If you want to begin to understand the way of Jesus, you must start to see people the way Jesus sees people. Jesus sees deeper than our behaviors. Sin has entered the world and cracked, not obliterated, the image of God in us. Christ sees the *tselem* in us. We must gain eyes to see the *tselem* in others, even our enemy-others. God's love in Christ operates well outside our lens of "Us vs. Them."

We are being called to imitate this kind of perfection in the world. This is why the apostle John says we will be known by our love (John 13:35), or conversely, "We will be known by our un-love" (paraphrase mine). So, we must ask ourselves: Are we resisting or submitting to the metaphysical force of love? Is our capacity to love all people growing or shrinking?

But There Is "Us," Right?

Part of our strong hesitancy to engage in love for our enemies is our inner sense of loyalty toward our own tribe. Galatians 6:10 says, "Therefore, as we have opportunity, let us do good to all people, especially to those who belong to the family of believers." We could emotionally interpret this verse in this way: "Therefore, first do good to the family of believers, then if you have any leftover, love all people" (paraphrase mine). We know how that works out. Many of us operate in a state of scarcity and feel we've only got so much love to go around. Do verses like this imply that there are levels of love? Not levels of love, but different kinds of love, for sure (see chapter 4).

I love my wife in a very *different* way than I love my next-door neighbor. I love those in my Christian community differently than I do the reading club at my local coffee shop. To love "them" on the other side of the fence does not cancel out the unique love you have for your nuclear family or spiritual family. The Trinity is a perfect example of this. The Father, Son, and Spirit are in an unending community (Us) of intimate love, and this love compels Them outward toward those unlike "Them." Yet, the love weaving the Trinity together in community is not diminished because of Their love for enemies. There is no way around it: to love those on the "them" side of the fence is a different kind of love, a love that stretches beyond our current relational fences.

US VS. THEM

We readily sort people into "Us" and "Them" based on the most arbitrary criteria. Of course, it's not only Christians that do this. We see ourselves as members of all sorts of tribes—our families, political parties, race, gender, social organizations. We even identify tribally based on our favorite sports teams— go Cowboys, go Yankees! Tribalism is pervasive, and it controls a lot of our behavior.

According to anthropologist Robin Dunbar, humans spend a majority of their conversations talking about the evil deeds of other people groups that are unlike them.[19] Tragic, but evidence that we define ourselves over and against others. While some rare individuals treat strangers like family, most of us see our small differences as a perfect excuse to bad mouth others. We don't have a lot of room to offer kindness or even a little benefit of the doubt to others unlike us.

It is an Us vs. Them time to be alive. But this is not a new story; it's actually an old story. From the time of the fall, the sin of contrast and comparison has plagued God's people—the tale of Cain and Abel, Jacob and Esau, the boys in the parable of the prodigal son.[20] Such examples are the product of the fall in Genesis 3 and do not come from God's original design for us in Genesis 1. A winner-takes-all political culture reinforces this sin in well-meaning Christians. Gun control, abortion, fracking, climate change, immigration, school vouchers, healthcare—the list of issues that cause us to be at each other's throats is endless.

We are to be known by love. Nothing less than the credibility of God's character is at stake if we are stingy and picky and selective with it. At this point, most conservatives love conservatives. Most progressives love progressives. And the two throw verbal grenades at each other from a distance over the fence. We are being invited into the way of Jesus that transcends these half measures of love.

Reflection Questions

1. What big idea about God's love lifts to the surface for you in this chapter?

2. What part of this love makes you feel uncomfortable or a bit conflicted?

3. What practical step can you take to embrace this *perfect* love in your life?

Chapter 3

HOW FEAR POLARIZES US

The process of categorisation is as old as man ... no other animal species categorises itself so neatly. ... [Yet it] is a process that destroys the very empathy that traditionally binds diverse communities together.

◆ JOSHUA KROOK

Fear compels us to run in the opposite direction when a grizzly bear wants to have us for lunch. Smart choice, right? Fear triggers our brain into action, saving us from distracted drivers or slick sales tactics. When something scares the daylights out of us, there are often two ways we deal with that scary thing: we attack it, or we avoid it. We are often pulled between these two responses.

It's never easy when someone accuses you of being someone you are not. Before the technology age, you'd find out

69

someone was peeved at you through the grapevine. Now you often find out by clicking a button. I clicked that button on a beautiful Monday morning. I was sipping my coffee, settled into my chapped leather chair, feeling the sunrise bliss, and made the mistake of checking my email.

What is that? The fabulous subject line—YOU ARE A LIAR—I should have stopped there, but I couldn't resist. Opening the email, the blowtorch of words was unleashed. Every adjective burnt me—"jerk, insensitive, dishonest, careless, power hungry, fake, manipulative"—you get the point. Come to find out, they had already started to plant sneaky and snarky seeds in the minds of some of our mutual friends. I closed my laptop because I thought it might overheat. I felt it; it was me against them. A sharp division. Two sides. I was good, they were bad. We were polarized. Is there any other option?

The two options most readily available to us are *attack* or *avoid*.[1]

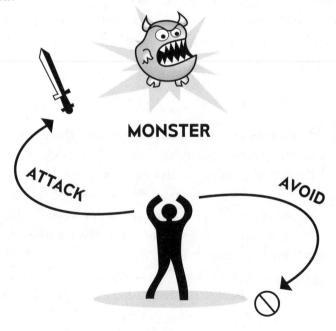

70

OPTION 1: ATTACK

We often identify with one action over another. For those who identify with Attack, we believe that this might be the only course of action that changes things. I wanted to blast off a response to that toxic email with my own slick-tongued counterattack. My wife convinced me to pause the email missile and launch it out the next day. That night I slept maybe five minutes. You know the crazy drill—you ruminate in your head on what you would say, what zingers could put the other person in their place. I imagined wrecking him with words. I began to stew in hatred. I started to hate him because I feared his ability to hurt me—lie about me, ruin my reputation, and humiliate me.

Some of us may unknowingly see the ministry of Jesus through this lens. Jesus was on a warpath to argue and destroy everything that resisted His purposes—He was a violent warrior. This was certainly what the Old Testament prophets seemed to describe and what many expected of the Messiah. This violent expectation is often the lens many read the book of Revelation with as well. There's no denying that the book of Revelation is full of violent imagery. But the literal interpretation of this imagery not only contradicts the Jesus of the Gospels and the teaching of rest of the New Testament, it also ignores the genre and historical context of this book and fails to pay close attention to how John uses apocalyptic symbolism.

It's profound that saints in Revelation overcome not with physical weapons but by "the blood of the Lamb" (Rev. 12:11), not by shedding other people's blood.[2] Along the same lines, it's significant that in the climactic battle scene of Revelation 19, the warrior Jesus is clothed with a blood-soaked robe *before* the battle even begins (19:13). The blood is clearly not that of His enemies, whom He has yet to fight. Rather, the symbolism suggests Jesus goes to battle and ultimately wins by shedding His own blood[3]—this is sacrificial love. In the face of His enemies, God in Christ does not attack in the way we might believe is necessary.

OPTION 2: AVOID

On the other hand, I was wondering how I could avoid responding to the email, dreaming about spotting them in the supermarket, dodging and hiding behind the towering display of Captain Crunch on sale for $2.99. One unhealthy way we cope with our fear is to retreat by finding people we agree with and limiting our relational connection to those we disagree with. We unfriend each other, limit our phone calls with that one uncle, and avoid certain people at church. Being "Minnesota Nice," having polite friendliness, or an aversion to confrontation isn't the answer either. This is a swampy space where we brew on our offenses, surrender to cowardice, and engage in passivity.

One unhealthy way we cope with our fear is to retreat by finding people we agree with and limiting our relational connection to those we disagree with.

Too often, we Christians switch between passive silence and bitter tirades in the face of differences. This is how passive-aggressive communication festers. "Passive" because one adopts the position of someone injured, and "aggressive" because one is covertly grasping for more power.[4] A passive-aggressive person judges another's motives without direct, open communication;

their relational strategy is indirectness so their anger cannot be identified but still felt. Pure passivity is not virtuous either, assuming that when someone insults us, the noble thing to do is roll over and play dead. Passive relating tends not to say anything in the moment of hurt but later vomits on someone unrelated to the situation.[5] This is dishonest relating. This was not the relational approach of Jesus.

For some reason, I thought I only had two options to keep my pride intact—*attack* or *avoid*. I was being swallowed up by polarization in my interpersonal relationship. Often without us knowing, the stress and fear we feel causes our brains to default to survival mode, bypassing the neocortex, the part of brain responsible for complex processing of empathy, patience, and curiosity. When we default to survival mode, we are not giving our brains time to change their cognitions in the face of fear.[6] We must slow down and move beyond our fear response that identifies anything unfamiliar or unusual as a monster. The only way to do this is hijack that cycle of Attack or Avoid. If your only option is to quickly lambaste or run in the opposite direction of everything that freaks you out, you have been polarized. Avoiding or attacking those who are unlike you or opposed to your beliefs will not lead you into healthy brain functioning and, more importantly, not into the way of Jesus.

Beyond Attack or Avoid

Recently a photo of Hillary Clinton and George W. Bush warmly embracing made its rounds and illustrated how polarization is fiercely forming the church. I found the picture moving to my pastoral heart. What saddened me was the visceral responses the picture elicited in both progressive and conservative Christians. Rather than being received as a picture of beauty in our ugly political landscape, it was received with anger. I heard many conservatives detest how Bush could embrace a "baby killer." I heard progressives abhor how Clinton hugged a "warmonger."[7] Before you stop here and start to argue who is worse, Bush or Clinton, we need to ask: Is there space for that type of connection, warmth, and proximity with each other when we are at odds? Can Clinton-types and Bush-types move beyond their fears and have affection for each other?

WHAT IS POLARIZATION?

Polarization creates two sharply contrasting groups or sets of opinions. We are aggressively shaped for polarization in our personal relationships as well as in our public politics—splitting us and pitting us against each other. It is an external force that tells us we only have two options—"our side" or "their side."

I remember a vivid moment of polarization at an early age. We had about nine friends in my neighborhood who played together all the time—backyard football, sliding on wet soapy tarps, playing hide-and-go-seek, and target practice with crab apples. One summer night, participating in our regular shenanigans at our local park, someone suddenly yelled that their Transformer was missing from their duffel bag. The blaming and finger-pointing began. Whatever subtle jealousies and antagonisms were already there came spewing to the surface like a violent volcano. My friends started immediately taking sides. Factions were quickly forming—four kids yelling and another four screaming back. I stood frozen as one kid called me out and said, "Dan, pick a side or go home." Sadly, that rift lasted for three years; we stopped playing together.

POLARIZATION AS A PRINCIPALITY

Polarization is a power or principality. As the apostle Paul says, "For we do not wrestle against flesh and blood, but against principalities, against powers . . . against spiritual hosts of wickedness in the heavenly places" (Eph. 6:12 NKJV). In his book *Engaging the Powers*, Walter Wink states that the language of "Principalities and Powers" in the New Testament refers to social dynamics that disunite humans from community, from creation, and from their Creator.[8] These divisive dynamics are what he calls "manifestations of the Enemy." The Enemy, Satan, has an agenda for this planet, an agenda for nations, for communities, for the church, for families, for every man, woman, and child—divide and destroy. Anyone versed in military tactics knows the maxim "divide and conquer." The Enemy delights in the strategy of turning us against each other, making us feel that accusing each other is much more practical.

Separating us has been the end goal of the Enemy since his initial destructive work in the garden of Eden. Adam and Eve are pitted against God, and Adam and Eve are pitted against each other—what once was together is separated. Deep down, we long to rewind and undo those choices made in utopia, but we also know we might have done the same. We feel the acidity in our gut. When we're unsatisfied with our current circumstance, we look to blame someone else—our spouse, our kids, our politicians, our spiritual leaders. There is something alluring and so natural about accusing others, clarifying an enemy when we're unsatisfied with life around us.

THE CATEGORIZER

Revelation 12:10 refers to Satan as "the accuser." Don't miss this. The Greek word for "accuser" is *categor*. This is where we get our English word "category." See what's going on? Satan is the eternal "categorizer." The eternal divider—ranking us, filing us, and fueling animosity between us. We blame, we label, we finger point, and somehow believe this fixes things. Do you find yourself categorizing the goodness or badness of people?

In contrast, togetherness has always been the eternal character of the Father, the Son, and the Spirit. They are in real relationship with each other. God is not sitting solo at an office desk somewhere in heaven, scribbling edicts on a notepad. God is a table of friends (Father, Son, and Spirit) sharing a cup of warm coffee, listening, conversing, and valuing each other's unique divine offerings. God's nature of perfect love is revealed in this dynamic relationship. They are mutually intertwined while also making room for each other—the world was born out of this. Togetherness is not a hippie idea—it's a holy idea. Satan labors to demolish and destroy this divine character in the world, in the church, and in you. Polarization is an external force generated by Satan.

Polarization has many faces, but it makes us see each other as monsters to fear, closing us down to each other, creating an Us vs. Them mentality, forcing us to categorize ourselves in contrast.[9]

Where do you feel this polarization?

When I was a kid, I remember that awkward feeling I had as my family drove past the Episcopal church on our way to our Baptist church. *What goes on in there?* I thought. There was a clear dividing line between us, the true Christians, and them . . . the fake Christians. To me as a kid, their big cathedral-looking church felt ominous compared to our building, which looked like a spruced up, nicely painted barn. No doubt they viewed us the same way with our weekly, pithy religious slogans displayed on our billboard.

One summer evening, our "Us vs. Them" played out for all to see. Our youth group walked down to the small park to grill some hot dogs and released teenagers to do what teenagers do. This time, the Episcopal youth group was stretching out all over our playground turf. What were they doing there? We didn't know what to do. Could we be near them? Should we be nice to them? Could we share our hot dogs with them? Somewhere in our hardly developed adolescent minds, we thought that being near them would do damage to our youth group. We felt self-protective fear. So we chose to avoid them. We were already polarized against each other, and we had never even met.

We naturally believed *their* sins were smellier than *our* sins. This is the same categorization we get caught up in when we engage our current political landscape. That "side" wants to kill babies, that "side" wants to enslave black folks, that "side" wants to dismantle the nuclear family, that "side" hates immigrants. We begin to believe that we are not evil like they are—their sins are worse than our sins. Or maybe we don't have any sins at all. We find a sense of superiority in our moral and political stances and move toward attacking or avoiding to soothe our fears.

Polarization takes people that have something in common, emphasizes their differences, hardens their differences into disgust, and slowly turns disgust into blatant hatred for each other.

Polarization takes people that have something in common, emphasizes their differences, hardens their differences into disgust, and slowly turns disgust into blatant hatred for each other.[10] They are heretical; we are orthodox. They are oppressors; we are liberators. They are immoral; we are righteous. It has become usual dialogue to identify how foolish, biased, dangerous, and illogical people are who do not think like "us," whichever side of "us" we are on.[11] We may blame politicians, news outlets, or activists—but they are just intermediaries. The Enemy plants the seed of polarization, but our own fears give vigorous life to it like fertilizer.

BEYOND US VS. THEM

Polarization starts early. As young ones, we see things simply. The world is divided into black and white, either/or. As children, it is difficult to identify with more than one view at a time.[12] Our brains have not developed to deal with the complexity of choice. I experienced this with my own son when he was three years old.

Our bedtime ritual was to read a story, snuggle, sing a song, and then I would look him in the eye and say, "I love you so much, buddy." Well, one night he responded with deep conviction: "I ONLY love momma. I don't love you. I just love momma!" After picking up my bleeding heart off the floor and attempting to put a Band-Aid on it, I gently responded, "You can love us both," and he would respond, "I can only love momma." This statement was his little psyche's way of attacking the tension of loving us both. This went on for nine months. He was afraid that if he chose to love me, he would lose his mom. And if he loved his mom, he would lose his dad. So he chose his mom for a season (maybe because she has softer skin . . . that's what I tell myself). Eventually, he grew out of that polarity and realized he could love us both. The late psychologist Carl Jung explained this phenomenon as one-sidedness.[13]

FALSE CHOICES

In our early development, we cannot comprehend tension, and it is something we try to eliminate. We like to live in a binary world where everyone is fundamentally "good" or "bad." But life isn't so cut and dried. Tension feels uncomfortable and unsafe. This polarized approach to relating with others can continue through adulthood, causing us to relate primarily in either/or, Us vs. Them categories.

When we see through a fear-based lens, it is effortless to think in terms of opposites with a false choice kind of logic: If something is this way, it cannot be that way.[14] But this isn't how the world is. For example, most people think that the opposite of white is black. But there are shades of black—from blackberries or blackbirds—that have nothing to do with white. The most beautiful moments are beyond the poles. When we see the blending of colors at dusk, or when the sea converges with the beach under our feet, or when we taste the salty and sweet mixed in that decadent dessert. Polarization constricts us to see, think, and feel along the lines of conflict, comparison, and clear lines. When you have a beautiful day out on the beach, you don't have to contrast it to going camping. Both can be beautiful experiences in different ways. We can grow up beyond polarized thinking, beyond placing everyone in categories of good or bad.

Does this mean we don't have opinions about what is right or wrong? Does God believe murder is wrong? Yes. Does

God believe lying is wrong? Yes. Does God believe slavery is wrong? Yes. Moving beyond the polarized lens does not preclude believing something is right or wrong. Yet, our primary lens for *seeing* people, and the ideas they hold, must move beyond that knee-jerk simplistic thinking. Henri Nouwen shared his own spiritual transformation: "The journey into the world, is a journey to find the Christ dwelling among us. God is in the world and we must move towards mystery, towards uncertainty into the interplay of the two sides battling. We must become alert to the cultural battle of good and evil and discover the mysterious mediating space."[15]

We are given false choices all the time, in which something is forcefully claimed to be an "either/or" situation, when in fact there is another, more creative option.[16] When my pals were fighting on the playground, I thought I only had two options. When our Baptist youth group encountered the Episcopal youth group, we thought we just had two choices: attack or avoid.

Certainly, seeing the world through only two choices is convenient and makes our life easier. But life is more of a spectrum of possible alternatives rather than an option between two extremes. Human nature, and subsequently Christianity and our cultural politics, consistently presents false choices. Like saying, "You are either with God or against God." Is this true? This type of speech offers us no room for the spectrum of journeying, exploring, and discerning. It certainly offers us security to think like this, but it is fundamentally not true to human experience nor does it echo the primary way Jesus related *with* humans. Be aware of how often you are given false choices, and how many times you give them to others.[17]

Here are a few examples:[18]

- I thought you cared about people, but you didn't call me back.

- If you don't memorize Scripture, you're not hiding God's Word in your heart.

- You either support this war, or you hate the military.

- If you don't support free health care, you're supporting the oppression of the poor.

- If you don't vote for the Republican candidate, you are supporting the murder of the unborn.

- You either support a Democrat for president, or you don't believe in women's rights.

The very nature of Christ Himself is beyond either/or. Is Jesus of Nazareth human or divine? Was He the Son of Man or the Son of God? He's both. Throughout church history, you can observe the church swing back and forth between these false choices. These are tactics that lock us inside a logical cage, but under closer scrutiny, there are more possibilities than an either/or choice. Black-or-white thinking doesn't allow for the many different variables, conditions, and contexts in which there would exist more than just the two possibilities put forth.[19] It frames the argument in ways as to create a side to take and therefore a people to fear.

ACTING LIKE CHILDREN

Part of Carl Jung's study was in human development and whether humans were willing and able to move beyond opposite poles and embrace tension and complexity in their life. He discovered that polarization is not a result of intellectual enlightenment or informed thinking; it is a result of emotional regression.[20] We slide back to childhood when we particularly fear something about a person or people group and deem it necessary to find ways to accumulate a burning mound of facts about why we should hate "them." Our primal brain (amygdala) takes over, convincing us there are only two options in polarized times—attack or avoid.[21] Let me say it plainly: when Christians respond in polarized ways, we are not growing up in Christ, we are acting as spiritual infants.

To live by the terms of polarization is to accept the immature perspective that there are only two poles to choose from. Since sin entered the world in Adam and Eve, we have been battling with a nature to move to one pole or another—Cain and Abel, Jacob and Esau, Jew and Gentile, Protestant and Catholic, conservative and progressive, friend or foe. We self-identify by our opposites, by our comparisons to the other pole of people. We see each other through comparison and opposition. This is why we use descriptive language of pretty/ugly, smart/stupid, success/failure, holy/unholy, not considering there are a hundred degrees between the two ends of each spectrum. This works well for the sake of simplification and argumentation, but not for the sake of loving others. So we inevitably label each other as the problem.

We tend to narrowly drift toward people who are like us and away from people who are not like us. The first moment a person meets another person, they are looking for a strategic difference that makes them better than the other person. Our human condition naturally falls into these fear-based patterns.

For Christians who believe in the existence of unchanging truth, an invitation to travel beyond left or right, good or bad, feels a bit like cruising down the slippery slope of wishy-washiness. And to Christians passionate about social justice, this seems milque-toast in the face of evil oppressors who hold power. This exact fear blinds us to the apostle Paul's ownership of thinking beyond the poles "we know in part and we prophesy in part" (1 Cor. 13:9) and that "for now we see through a glass, darkly" (1 Cor. 13:12 KJV).

HUMBLE OPINIONS

Imagine you are standing in the middle of a vast forest, or at least that's what it seems like. That forest represents truth, all truth. You cannot see the whole forest, but you can see around you. This is your purview on truth. The more you walk through the forest, the more you see, the more truth you take in. You see a mighty oak tree and think, *I must be in Texas. It's blistering hot, and that's where Goose Island State Park is with all the oak trees.* But you walk for another hour and see vast ridges and rocks and think, *Maybe I'm in Virginia, in the summer, the Blue Ridge forest has lots of oak trees.* The farther and longer you walk the more you see, the more your knowledge of where you are is filled out. You climb up a long trail, get above the tree line, and see the coast. *Am I in California, in the oak woodlands?*

This is the truth—you don't see all there is to see from the spot you are standing in. Paradoxically, the more you see, the more you know, but also the more humbled you become. The wiser we become, the less wise we feel. This is the wellspring of intellectual humility—the more you know, the less you realize you know. So, embrace some fallibility with your opinions. This is the tension that a nonpolarized view of others embraces. I don't know all, I don't see all, and that's okay. I am not dumb, weak, or wishy-washy because of it. It does not mean I don't hold some beliefs as truth; I just hold them with less blunt force. I invite you to walk through the forest of life, humbly, not as one making either/or statements on everything and everyone you see.

Did Jesus dwell with people beyond the polarizing posture of either/or?

DID JESUS TAKE SIDES?

We feel we must take a side. This is the gravitational pull of polarization. If we do not take a side, we fear we'll be left standing in the pathetic middle, nobody will like us, and we'll be in the wrong. We're convinced that Jesus, like us, sees the world through the lens of "baddies" and "goodies." Make no mistake, Jesus inhabited a polarized culture in the first century that had many spicy divisions.

You are probably familiar with the Pharisees. The Pharisees receive the most negative press in the New Testament and are often portrayed as "the bad guys." The Pharisees were meticulous observers of the ancestral laws, taking a literal view of their interpretation. They were most concerned with exact obedience to God's laws to bring about the kingdom for the Jews. Pharisees kept their hands clean from most civic engagements and instead engaged in affairs that concerned the temple religious system.[22] Pharisees might be parallel to certain fundamentalist brands of conservative Christians today.

The Essenes were another group of people very concerned with purity and ritual.[23] Their concern for purity led them to be isolationist as they shared in communal property and bound themselves to moral vows. Many Essenes were celibate, believing sex defiled their holiness before God.[24] A portion of them was so concerned about temple purity that they would not go in at all. It's possible to see some overlap with the Essenes of Jesus' day and the Amish and other groups today that isolate for the sake of sectarian purity.

The Sadducees, a Jewish sect, were another formal political movement in the first century. They were often in heated contention with the Pharisees. The Sadducees did not believe in the authoritative nature of the Mosaic laws.[25] They denied the resurrection of the dead, activity of angels, and host of other supernatural things. Sadducees had a much more figurative than literal interpretation of God's law. The Sadducees seemed to have been characterized by civic engagement. Sadducees had a less contentious relationship with the Roman establishment as they oversaw many affairs of the state, collecting taxes, and setting up a judicial system in the towns. They were probably more akin to progressive Protestants.

The Zealots were another movement that took their religious understanding of Judaism and turned that into a political agenda, seeking to incite rebellion against the Roman Empire and expel it from the Holy Land. The Zealots had a significant following among the poor. They believed that the Roman Empire was oppressive and should be overthrown. The Zealots' interpretation of the law was deeply rooted in the exodus out of Egypt. They were probably more akin to Occupy Wall Street types of groups.

The Sicarii were another political group that was a branch of the Zealots. The Sicarii believe God could and would use violence to liberate the oppressed.[26] Egypt oppressed the marginalized, and God liberated them violently through the plagues and the drowning of the Egyptian army in the Red Sea. Some of them were willing to be violent, even beating and bludgeoning other Jews who cooperated in business with the

Roman Empire. They were probably more akin to Antifa or abortion clinic bombers.

The vast majority of Jews sympathized and aligned with one of these political groups. Each political group debated each other in the temple courts and markets, declaring their position as the truth. Sounds scary close to our current times, even without CNN and Fox News, doesn't it?

THE GREAT DISRUPTER

Why did the gospel of Luke choose to begin with firsthand accounts of what four people expected the Messiah to look like? Why did God deem it essential to share the messianic predictions of Mary, Zechariah, Simeon, and John the Baptist? In part, Luke's inclusion of these four messianic descriptions helps us realize that most envisioned a different kind of messiah than the kind Jesus turned out to be. Though each of them had pieces of who they thought King Jesus would be, He would not become their puppet. Jesus did not play by the rules of any political parties of His day. Jesus was frequently pressured by people to fit into a category. Everyone had political or religious agendas they placed on Jesus, and He frustrated them with divine delight.

To the Pharisees, Jesus will not abide by the strict application of God's law. To the Sadducees, Jesus defies their belief in a nonsupernatural world. To the Essenes, Jesus embraces being with uncleanness. To the Zealots, Jesus will not use His power to overthrow the tyrannical Empire. To the Sicarii, Jesus did not use violence to accomplish justice. Jesus is stretching our imaginations beyond the polarization-box we're stuck in. If you want to know about the Jesus-movement, look at its strategic start. When Jesus gathered the first disciples, it was a scandal.

THE SCANDAL

A scandal gets at our instinctual core and demands more than a cursory acknowledgment. The Bible uses the word scandal (*skandalon* in Greek) to explain the emotional impact of Jesus. A scandal is something that simultaneously attracts and repels. We typically associate a scandal with something naughty and negative. Jesus scandalized our world, disrupting our framework of polarization—the "Us vs. Them" categories, the either/or responses, the simplistic side-taking we revert to. Jesus was pioneering a new way, ancient wisdom—one that applies both to playground disputes and political conflicts. As Jesus engaged real people and faced real systems, He did not meet the blunt force of fear with opposing fear. The world around us is aching for this alternative the path beyond attacking or avoiding, and the feelings of repulsion we feel toward each other.

This scandal can feel jarring. Imagine two teams are playing the classic game tug-o-war. Pulling, grinding, digging in their heels. The sweat is rolling down their faces, the grunts from the pain of rope-burned hands, and exhausted from pulling. Teammates are yelling at each other to yank harder. This is what polarization does—it locks us into battle. But suddenly you walk up without anyone noticing and take a pair of giant shears and cut the middle of the rope. Snap! Everyone crashes to the ground. For a second, each team thinks they beat the other team. Eventually, they realize nobody won. The raging energy of things—the plans, the agendas, and the habits we find ourselves cemented in—Jesus *scandalizes* it all. Everyone was pulling for their side to win, caught in a power struggle.

LOVE HOLDS THE SPACE

In the selection of His disciples, Jesus gathered three Zealots who were militant nationalists, a tax collector who favored the Sadducee party, six fishermen who lived hand-to-mouth and were exploited by Roman taxation, one member of the Sicarii party,[27] and a wealthy nobleman who was linked to the Pharisees.[28] This is scandalous! It's like organizing a home church with a few Black Lives Matter protesters, blue-collar workers who believe Donald Trump will fix the country, a couple on public assistance while working for minimum wage at McDonald's, a wealthy Republican gentleman who owns an oil refinery down South, and a member of Antifa. It's an understatement to say these men would have loathed being in the same room with each other.

If it were not for Jesus holding this space, they'd all naturally slide into the cultural ditch of mutual hatred for one another. He called them into the same inner circle, a space that would demand something from everyone. Jesus sits with the progressive—the Jameses and Johns who are zealous to see God's kingdom restore justice to oppressed people. Jesus also sits and shares meals with the Matthews—a tax collector who had cozied up to the occupying powers (some might consider him a greedy neocon). Jesus traveled with them in close quarters, ate with them, interrupted debates between them, and modeled to them a love that defied political affiliations. With deep affection, He calls them friends (John 15:15). As the disciples faced each other day after day, ideological and relational differences emerged. Jesus lives and moves and breathes beyond fear—He invites us to do the same.

Jesus purposely disrupted the social lines and political boundaries that fear builds between "us and them." Jesus was not supposed to speak to the woman at the well. He is a Jew, and she is a Samaritan—they are expected to be enemies. Jesus was not supposed to show kindness to Roman soldiers, because they were the oppressors who used the sword to control—they were expected to be enemies. Jesus was not supposed to spend time with prostitutes. They

The very makeup of Jesus' first discipleship group was a purposeful message about the kingdom of God—Jesus was starting a polarization-busting movement.

were viewed as unclean—they were expected to be enemies. Jesus was not supposed to share a meal with a tax collector. They cheated the poor out of their hard-earned wages—they were expected to be enemies.

Did Jesus care about social justice? Of course.

Did Jesus care about morality and righteousness? Of course.

But something else was superior, more powerful.

The very makeup of Jesus' first discipleship group was a purposeful message about the kingdom of God—Jesus was starting a polarization-busting movement. Jesus was cultivating a thick space of transformation, rejecting the arrangements that fear creates. When someone offends us, frightens us, votes differently than us, or seeks to betray us, we all feel the drag into polarization—to pick a side. The left-right seesaw is a snare of the Enemy, it is a delusion—reject it altogether. Jump off the seesaw, let Jesus scandalize you.

CHOOSING ANOTHER MAP

I once had to make my way across an unfamiliar city with a GPS. It ended up taking me straight into a construction zone where all the streets were shut down. I did not know any route other than the one dictated to me by my GPS, and it kept re-routing me back into the same construction zone. I knew there must be another way to get to the other side of the city, but my GPS only had one route. Fear can be viewed as the fuel that runs the car, and polarization can be considered the GPS map we're told to follow. In a polarized culture, we are offered only one set of directions when we fear someone or something—one that leads us into side-taking, pitted against one another. It's the only route our culture views as viable.

I was tempted to toss my GPS out the window, smashing it on the street—we do not have to accept the conditions that our culture of polarization dictates to us. Polarization is destroying the witness of God's love in our lives. Polarization is not a necessary evil to tolerate—it's a fear-based evil to obliterate.

If we want to understand Jesus, the One who began it all, we must be scandalized by how He dwelt beyond the polarities, how His teaching unravels "Us vs. Them" postures.

If we want to understand Jesus, the One who began it all, we must be scandalized by how He dwelt beyond the polarities, how His teaching unravels "Us vs. Them" postures to being with people. Jesus spoke firmly against sexual immorality but was also very comfortable gaining a reputation for hanging out with sexually immoral folks (Matt. 11:19; Luke 7:34).

Throughout His ministry, Jesus prophetically spoke against oppression but then encourages an impoverished and socially rejected woman to pour a full years' worth of her wages on His feet (Mark 14:6–9). The disciples are astounded at the recklessness of this act. Jesus tells them "the poor you will always have with you."

Don't overspiritualize these actions. Conservatives today would be saying "Jesus is a liberal" in their blog posts because Jesus sometimes appears ambiguous due to His willingness to associate with sexually immoral people. On the other side, you'd have progressives outraged, starting a hashtag, and calling out Jesus for making moral judgments and taking advantage of an impoverished woman. We need a new map for engaging one another.

NEW WINESKINS

Jesus was concerned with something much more important than being clear about His associations, taking sides, and protecting His reputation. Jesus is piloting a new scandalous space for the practice of love, a perfect love, a whole love. This is not a neutral or passive work. As we'll discover in the next chapter, it is the most costly, risk-taking work. Fear tells us to stay away—we can only dwell with those who vote like us, look like us, and dig what we dig.

Jesus calls this "old wineskins." It is the voice of fear seeking to be the primary container of our emotions—keeping the kindness of God bottled up in our own tribe. So, it communicates with physical and emotional sensations of discomfort, which we don't like to acknowledge as fear. It commands that we live by guttural responses without asking questions. We are living in agitated times. You probably observe this on your social media feed and in heated conversations at Thanksgiving. We tend to rely on emotional reactions rather than contemplative responses.[29]

Jesus points out that "old wineskins" cannot hold any new wine. New wine is often still fermenting so it should be placed in new containers (often made of goatskins). When skins are still fresh, they are pliable and expandable and can handle the active nature of the wine. Old wineskins though have dried to a point that they will no longer expand. Placing new wine in old wineskins is a disaster, "the new wine will burst the skins; the wine will run out and the wineskins will be ruined" (Luke 5:37–38).

Fear cannot contain what God's Spirit desires to pour inside us. It cannot carry "faith working through love" (Gal. 5:6 NKJV). Jesus is calling His followers out of fear-based ways of relating with each other. There is a new map, a way beyond *attacking* or *avoiding* our enemies—the way of *affection*.

Reflection Questions

1. What about the concept of polarization is new to you in this chapter?

2. What part of "false choices" makes you feel some conflict or confusion?

3. What practical step can you take to move beyond either/or ways of relating with others?

Chapter 4

AFFECTION FOR MONSTERS

Men think that it is impossible for a human being to love his enemies, for enemies are hardly able to endure the sight of one another. Well, then, shut your eyes—and your enemy looks just like your neighbor.

◆ SØREN KIERKEGAARD

Beyond the edges of maps, where explorers had not yet traveled, imaginations ran wild that medieval monsters existed. Tales and stories of fantastical creatures—some prowled in faraway lands, others lurked closer to home, and they created an ever-present threat to ordinary folk in medieval times. Strange beasts appeared in literature, crept into sermons at church, were argued about in the public square, and peppered discussion at dinner parties. Monsters hovered in the background of the medieval mindset.

The folklore of these monsters was often about humans who had deformed into beasts, such as the Panotii, which had huge ears for wings; or the Hircocervus, which was part deer, part goat, and part human; or the Sea Monk, which was a mix between a fish and a man supposedly living in the seas around Denmark.[1] So much of the planet was mysterious to them. In many ways, this was how they made sense of the depths of the world and hazards of the unknown.

I love the drawings of these medieval creatures—they are crude renderings, catching facets of human beauty but contrasted with grotesque horror. They capture the way we see our universal human consciousness. We can look at medieval people's belief in real monsters as ignorant, but rather, these creatures served a specific role in their culture. This was how they faced the unfamiliar, what was beyond their understanding.[2] Monsters acted as anti-humans, allowing them to better define themselves against that which was odd. Monsters were evil, dangerous, grotesque, and provided an example of what they were not.

Source: Jacob van Maerlant, *Der Naturen Bloeme*, Flanders, ca. 1350. Wikimedia Commons. Public domain.

WE BELIEVE IN MONSTERS

While we are indeed more enlightened and sitting on mounds of education in the twenty-first century, we still create monsters lurking in the world. The more we talk about "them," the bigger their fangs are, the more bloodthirsty, and the more we feel our lives are at risk.

Those things that annoy us, offend us, or seem straight up bananas to us can morph into monsters. Things we ruminate on over and over, online, on cable news, and in the echo chamber of our minds. We make monsters of people; it helps us define ourselves—our own goodness and their badness.

We are being beckoned beyond *avoidance* and beyond *attacking* in the face of those things that frighten us and then polarize us. There is a more scandalous way. Jesus invites us onto the path of *affection*, affection for monsters. I have deep affection for my wife, my kids, and my friends. But affection for monsters? Really?

Affection is a visceral, tangible, crowding-your-space type of word. I'm probably not the only one who felt a little embarrassed and weird if they saw their parents getting all touchy and close while dancing in the kitchen to "Love Me Do" by the Beatles. Seeing affection profoundly connects with us. To be affectionate one must choose vulnerability in a volatile world, and this is why it sticks out like someone wearing shorts on a winter day. Affection touches us on an existential level. I get a little charge of emotion when I see two senior citizens sitting in a restaurant, sipping on a glass of wine, holding hands across the table. Affection is powerful, sacred even. This is probably why we reserve it for people we really like, not for people we really loathe. When it comes to people we don't like (you know who they are), the last thing you want to do is show affection.

OPTION 3: AFFECTION

Now when Jesus saw the crowds, he went up on a mountainside and sat down. His disciples came to him, and he began to teach them. . . . "You have heard that it was said, 'Love your neighbor and hate your enemy.' But I tell you, love your enemies and pray for those who persecute you, that you may be children of your Father in heaven. He causes his sun to rise on the evil and the good and sends rain on the righteous and the unrighteous. If you love those who love you, what reward will you get? . . . And if you greet only your own people, what are you doing more than others? Do not even pagans do that? Be perfect, therefore, as your heavenly Father is perfect." (Matt. 5:1, 43–48)

These words of Jesus are perplexing. On the one hand, we can recognize that if all humanity acted according to these words, our world and our relationships would be infinitely better.[3] At the same time, they seem entirely foolish. "Try this method of love on a tiger and see what will happen," was said by writer Eli Stanley Jones.[4] Jones is illustrating the seeming foolishness we all feel when it comes to showing any level of affection to enemies. Positively, this method does not influence tigers, but might it affect humans?

In our imaginations, we presuppose that within every battle there are two beings: one who is evil and fights with cruelty, and another who is not evil and is being assaulted by the cruel. That most likely was the context for these verses. There was a common understanding among first-century Jewish folks who "the enemy" was. The "enemy" was the Roman occupier they suffered under, who cheated them out of their wages and utterly disregarded justice. These words "love your enemies" proclaimed by Jesus are defining love not as a hypothetical situation but as a prescription in the worst of conditions. To love, or even like, your enemy seems to be impossible for most of us, even if the enemy is only a next-door neighbor making too much noise after 10 p.m. However, this is what Jesus was calling for in the Sermon on the Mount, and today, this ethical demand changes everything.

Loving people is hard; it is a beautiful burden. Loving unlovable people is particularly difficult. But loving your enemy? As much as I would like to assemble a list of caveats to excuse away enemy-love, Jesus doesn't.[5] The Greek word for enemy (*echthroi*) is often used in the broadest sense to include religious, political, and personal enemies. The word *echthroi* is used often in the New Testament to refer to military enemies. This love Jesus is speaking about called its hearers to imagine the worst enemies in their life that harassed and hurt them.

Who might those people be for you?

LOOKING FOR LOOPHOLES

In the same context, Jesus compares loving our enemies to the Father's love for all people: the "just and on the unjust" (Matt. 5:45 NKJV). Why does Jesus qualify "just" and "unjust"? Jesus knows how we like to place qualifiers on our love, you know, find the loophole. There is nothing in Jesus' words that restricts the meaning of "enemy" to certain types of people. Jesus' call to love our enemy is indistinguishable; it extends to every last person on the planet. Other religions teach that people should love their neighbors. They even teach forgiveness for those who wronged them. But loving your enemy? Only Jesus takes our engagement with our enemies this far. This is how far the love of God extends to us—"while we were God's enemies" Christ loved us. Jesus' command to love our enemies matches His own love for enemies.

The glory of God's love is the radical journey Christ took

to win us over. Listen, I would journey over land, sea, and even go to the dentist to love my wife and kids, but my enemies? That's the point of "If you love those who love you . . . ?" (Matt. 5:46; Luke 6:32). Most everyone would do that. But this love Jesus is talking about breaks that boundary.

Rather than *attacking* us with judgment or *avoiding* us through abandonment, God moves toward us with *affection*. God likes us, loves us, even when we don't like Him or love Him. We are polarized against God, but Christ builds a bridge of kindness with His own body. Jesus is inviting us to do something He did Himself; He's no hypocrite. This passage is eliminating the way we categorize our neighbors and enemies differently. Our "categorizing" allows us to love our neighbors and hate our enemies. The way of Jesus transcends the law of equivalence and introduces a new commandment. Jesus is telling us that the abundance of love must not be overpowered by the logic of hate.

We are being taught every day how to hate our enemies rather than how to love them. We are told the world is more dangerous. The assault on our values is imminent. The enemy is out there—just check your social media feed. A frenzy of clickbait and terrifying headlines scream at us from our media sources. Over-the-top, attention-grabbing statements capture our eyes to rise above the competition. Fear is far more contagious than love, and now we have the perfect digital network through which to spread it far and wide.

The art of hating our neighbors is the skill taught by both the conservative powers and the progressive powers. They are all attempting to capture your most scarce resource—your attention—and take it hostage with the language of fear. They stoke our innate anxiety, conveniently offering us someone to focus our hatred on, to turn into a monster.

We need a sober evaluation of the strategies used on us: your preferred political party is teaching you how to hate, to zealously believe that the biggest problems we face as a society are a result of the monsters on the other side of the fence. The allure of hatred is badgering and bullying us everyday.[6] We are made to think that grinding in hatred toward your enemies is necessary to eliminate the threats.

Through the words, works, and ways of Jesus, we are being swept up into God's love for all people. Jesus is revealing the uncomfortable specifics of this kind of love; it is enemy-love. This kind of love is foreign to our current culture of competition. Many of the people Jesus encounters are looking for the asterisk, the exceptions, as we often do. I often wonder if the disciples pulled Jesus aside and gave Him a long list of hypotheticals for why affection for enemies wouldn't work. Every time I mention enemy-love in the midst of polarizing times the responses are always "Yeah, but what about . . ."

LOVING NEIGHBOR BUT HATING ENEMIES

On another occasion, Jesus is asked about the greatest commandment. He replies, "'Love the Lord your God with all your heart and with all your soul and with all your mind'" (Matt. 22:37). But this is too vague, too nice, too easy to plug into a worship song or mission statement. Jesus qualifies His answer to love God by adding a twist that redefines the whole thing: "And the second is like it: 'Love your neighbor as yourself'" (v. 39). So typical of Jesus—stirring the pot. He couples these two truths and starts to create a "whole" love, a perfect love.

The lawyer's follow-up question reveals the heart, my heart, your heart. "Who is my neighbor?" Or as modern-day

Christians may ask, "Jesus—exactly who do I have to treat as worthy of love?" That's when Jesus chooses to tell the story of the Good Samaritan. Why tell this story? Just a bit of cultural background: at the time of Jesus, Samaritans lived amongst Jews in modern-day Israel, but the two groups did not intermingle with each other.[7] They hated one another. The feelings were mutual. The story is defined by two groups who don't value each other and consider each other morally wrong.

The story of the Good Samaritan is enticing people into deeper listening, to seek hidden meaning that requires a sincere effort of their imagination. I submit to you that the majority of Christianity, as we know, is really okay with the vagueness of "love your neighbor"; it gives us space to feel the good feelings of love without the gritty qualities of this story.[8] To help our imaginations, the story could be rephrased for us to elicit the feelings it elicited back then: "The Good Progressive" or "The Good Conservative."

The majority of Christianity, as we know, is really okay with the vagueness of "love your neighbor"; it gives us space to feel the good feelings of love without the gritty qualities.

The question "who is my neighbor?" lobbed at Jesus implies that the lawyer believes he has a choice. Maybe I can choose who to love? We prefer sentimental love, one that gives us a choice to embrace the map of polarization. Christians are notorious for loving people on their terms, in their buildings, with their programs, with their branding.

As Jesus tells the story, the "enemy" in the passage (the Samaritan) is moved toward *affection*, literally "moved in his innards" at the sight of his enemy in misery. This is what God invites us into as well, to feel it in our innards, to feel it in every particle of our being—affection. Everything turns on affection as the poet and novelist Wendell Berry once said.

> The imagination thrives on contact, on tangible connection. For humans the imagination enables empathy, empathy enables affection. And it is in affection that we find the possibility of neighborly and kind connections with each other. . . . The charge will be made that affection is an emotion, merely "subjective," and therefore is reserved for the things we love most, our children and our automobiles, not for things we deem less important . . . but choosing affection for difficult places and difficult people raises the worth of those things that we imagined as less worthy. . . . Everything turns on affection.[9]

Loving our enemies is affection—a movement of warm hospitality rather than warring hostility. We humans learn the real act and art of love as we choose affection for "difficult" people. We allow love that flows into us from God to soak our being, to then flow out from our whole heart, mind, and strength. We experience the affection of God, and it energizes affection for our enemies.

Jesus is messing with the lines of Us vs. Them. Your neighbor is whoever's manner of life you exceptionally dislike. Whose personhood is across the void socially, ethnically, politically, culturally. When you look at their morals, their practices, their beliefs, you dry heave just a little. To recall my biker neighbor across the street, I suspected he was a politically opinionated, womanizing, chain-smoking bro. He was, and my innards were moved toward antipathy rather than affection. I sense the disciples felt this hearing the story of the Samaritan. Why? Jews hated Samaritans more than Romans, the same way some Republicans hated President Obama more than bin Laden or some Democrats hate Trump more than Putin.[10] Jesus is bringing the scandal of the gospel into the light for all to see. The spark of enemy-love can set the world afire.

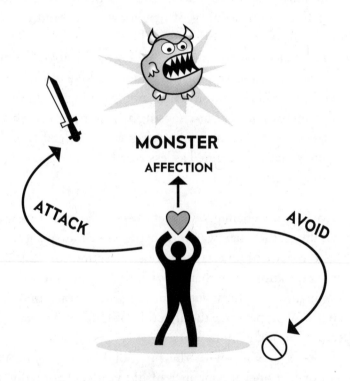

THE WORK OF AFFECTION

Locally I've been able to watch the practice of affection for our enemies unfold. With the help of a peacemaking initiative in my neighborhood, a cluster of people were brought together for a three-month Police and Community Dialogue of sharing a meal, swapping stories, and working through hostility. This was a place-based community experiment that understood that there was the elephant in the room—neighborhood residents and the police force had deep fear of each other. There was a faction growing between those two groups in my neighborhood. A diverse cross-section of people were pulled together—a white female professor, a Republican business owner, an unemployed Hispanic woman with two kids, a Middle Eastern man, a black homeless gentleman, a longtime black social worker, and my wife, a white, educated church planter. As these neighborhood residents came together, three police officers joined as well for the dialogue.

A mediator led discussions on racism, violence, religion, governance, and our neighborhood history. Every week was filled with spicy dialogue; contentious labels were tossed around, disagreements were clarified. But something slowly grew in the gaps between neighbor to neighbor, and neighbor to police officer. Where there was antagonism and automatic anger, something more shocking started to sprout up—affection. A black man shared with officers his experience of being pulled over, bullied around, and assumed to have already done something because of his skin color. He shared through tears of pain what it was like to see an officer come his way, raw and real. One officer began to shed tears; he had no idea. He asked insightful questions to find out more. A connection began to form between that white officer and that black man. They even decided to go out and get a cup of coffee together.

Another officer shared about his time in the neighborhood, the panic attacks, the times he'd thought he'd never come home to his family again. The violence and blood he saw, the PTSD he was embarrassed to share that he had. Something began to uncork in the room. The homeless gentleman shared he had panic attacks as well. They stumbled into moments of common humanity. After consecutive weeks sharing meals and stories, the officers and residents were so vulnerable that the Republican small-business owner said: "I feel like I found some new brothers and sisters."

This is no small work: getting enemies to move beyond their fears to develop affection for each other. Jesus modeled these boundary-crossing conversations—latent with the surprise of kindness, and healing. This is ultimately the work of enemy-love.

LOVING MONSTERS IN THE OLD TESTAMENT

Affection for enemies might seem absent in the Old Testament. But if we look closely, we can see little beams of light that point to the revolutionary words of Jesus. The most iconic character in the Old Testament, Jonah, reveals to us the psychological struggle of loving enemies. Jonah from beginning to end, is repelled, like I was, by this journey of showing affection to his enemies.

The story of Jonah makes for a great children's mural on the Sunday school class wall. The big blue ocean, the cute gray big fish, and little ole Jonah hanging out inside its belly. I was told the tale of Jonah as a kid, and in my imagination, the belly of the big fish had a rocking chair, a table with an open Bible resting on it, and a candle flickering in the dark. I think I imagined it that way because the story seemed like a sweet moral folktale. If you disobey God, He might send a fish to gobble you up, but if you pray, He'll let you out—really clear and straightforward. We've turned this story into a bedtime story, but there is something more ominous and profound going on.

As we meet Jonah, we may not realize that he is the only

prophet who runs from his assignment.[11] Every prophet in Scripture jumps on board, but not Jonah. Many of the prophets had some disturbing orders: take a prostitute as a wife, or build a massive ark, lay on your side naked for 390 days, eat a scroll, and many other crazy antics. Something about this directive frightens Jonah to his core and sends him running away. What was he doing when God came to him with this fear-laden job assignment?

We don't find the answer in the book of Jonah; for that we have to go to 2 Kings. It records Jonah's significant influence in the life of Israel's political life. We discover that Jonah is part of the restoration of the border wall of Israel from Lebo-hamath to the Sea of Arabah. Track with this: Jonah is leading the initiative to construct a wall of protection.[12] This wall was all that stood between their neighbors to the north. And who were those neighbors? The Assyrians.

The Assyrian army was a war machine, and they were on Israel's doorstep. The fear of falling into their hands was extreme. They had been plundered and pillaged by them before "for Israel was afflicted, for there was none left, bond or free." The prophet Nahum records Assyria's reputation saying "Woe to the city of blood, full of lies, full of plunder, never without victims!" (Nah. 3:1). They were a brutish empire in the ancient world. They treasured violence as they built towers out of the bones and skulls of the tribes they conquered.[13] The King of Nineveh was the tyrant of the land. He had built a great city, an epicenter of commerce, by punishing every tribe around it.

Jonah and his people had experienced Assyria's salivating taste for death and destruction. I'm sure Jonah had wept over the loss of friends and family by their hands. No wonder Jonah is building a wall between the beaten down Hebrew people and their empire. Can you imagine what Jonah felt toward these monsters: fear, malice, disgust, teeth-grinding hate. This is no longer a quaint children's story; it's a Quentin Tarantino film.

The irony is unavoidable that Jonah is building a wall to fight an oppressive enemy, and God calls him to put down his sword and shovel to go be *with* them. It seems absurd to respond to such a monster without armed resistance, but by going and talking things over—at least it does to me. The last thing I want to do in the face of those I fear is to show them any level of affection.

Feel the visceral connection with Jonah. God wants to show compassion for a people who had subjected them to atrocities. The character of God's love is being revealed.

When we hear "love your enemies," we tend to domesticate it and turn it into thinking nice thoughts about people who've been mean to us. Ultimately the space between us will dominate our best intentions. Attempts at nice ideas will turn to ill-will and uncharitable judgments. The story of Jonah and the story of the Good Samaritan are not about sending nice thoughts from a distance. They are both tales of touch, of feel, of affectionate-action toward another we perceive as a monster.

THE VOID BETWEEN US

Fear thrives in the void, in the distance between us. We worship our opinions, our convictions, and our political perspectives. They have become a Grand Canyon between us.[14] The more distances we create from what we fear, the more polarization solidifies as our map for relating. It's quite amazing how we interpret insurmountable conflict into the void; the nothingness between us.

Recently an acquaintance posted on their Facebook feed that "Refugees are rapists." My interest was piqued because my wife and I have spent hundreds of hours caring for refugees in our city. We have shared meals with beautiful folks from the Congo, Burma, Syria, and Afghanistan. We've listened to gut-wrenching stories of families fleeing genocide and mothers watching their children starve. We've personally never met a refugee-rapist. I'm sure they exist, as do American rapists, if that is the sloppy language we are using. I called my acquaintance cold turkey. He was shocked I called him. Gently, I asked if he had any friends who are refugees, followed by stammering and silence on the end of the line. He confessed his opinion was based on internet research. "Did your research included any interpersonal presence?" My suggestion was that he suspend his opinion until he had at least attempted to close the void relationally. I invited him to come visit, share a meal, and meet my refugee friends. We often fill the void with fear, and fear wants to create monsters out of image-bearers.

My all-time favorite movie as a kid was *The NeverEnding Story*. The main villain in the book and the film is "the Nothing." It is a frightening dark cloud that nearly engulfs the magical world of Fantasia. Only a child with an imagination of hopefulness and innocent joy can dispel it. The Nothing represents cynicism, fear, and a loss of wonder. In the novel, the Nothing is an inconceivable, formless, featureless monster, impossible to describe and define. When Atreyu (one of the protagonists) attempts to look at it, he cannot process what stands before his eyes. It is a destructive presence that engulfs everything, devouring all the space in the world. It is an unusual force that, instead of leaving carnage in its wake, leaves a void.

This is what polarization does to us—creates a void, a massive distance, a formless fear between us. Both with the story of Jonah and the story of the Good Samaritan, God is showing us that the void must be reduced for love to spring up between us.

When there is a void of relational connection, people naturally start to assume the worst and suspect dark motives. Something nefarious sprouts, and the labels begin to flow: they are immoral, they are racists, oppressors, Marxists, heretics . . . they are _____. We lock one another into cages our labels build. My Facebook friend made a judgment because of a void between him and the refugees he feared. He filled it in with detached research and reckless caricatures. He turned refugees into enemies.

CONNECTION LOST

Let me tell you how to be the laughingstock of your next dinner party—challenge the presumption that technological progression is a good thing. Other than a few head nods about how we really should unplug from our devices for a few minutes a day, you will likely be scoffed at as a backwoods hermit.

Hailed as the great unifier that would bring people together, technology has created a void between us. Indeed, modern technology enables us to plug into anything happening in the world, but are we more connected to each other? It seems to be making us more frayed than ever before and strangely more secluded from empathizing with others unlike us. Modern technologies optimize convenience and speed, giving us an astonishing ability to share ideas, literature, art, and music. But if rates of anxiety and the disintegration of social bonds are our guides, our fragile souls cannot handle what is occurring to us. Studies are showing that the more connected we are to the virtual world, the less relationally attached we are to each other.[15]

We are now a generation linked to a Twitter and Facebook understanding of human interaction. No matter how well we defend the ingenious ways that technology connects us, we

110

know, in our heart that something is amiss. We know that all our online connections cannot equal one real person sitting next to us, listening to our life story, embracing our presence, and just being there physically.

It hasn't always been this way. In the Near Eastern world of the Bible in the first century, the world was primarily oral. Obviously, you are reading this book, so at some point, the printing press pushed us to establish that the written word become a new point of connection.[16] We are now in an era in history when so much of our relating is mediated by technology—email, text, Twitter, etc. Our five senses of touch, taste, smell, sight, sound are quickly being traded in for blogs, 280 characters, comment sections, virtual reality, and emojis. Our full arsenal for connecting as humans is slowly being sidelined for convenience. This has made our social circles increasingly narrow and more tribal.

All our online connections cannot equal one real person sitting next to us, listening to our story, embracing our presence, and just being there physically.

Based on the most extensive study of US political attitudes ever undertaken by the Pew Research Center, a social force is aggressively ordering us into "siloing"—the tendency to interact mostly with like-minded people: 28% of people say that "it's important to live in a place where most people share my political views." Similarly, 63% of those described as "consistently conservative" say most of their close friends share their worldview, while 49% of those who are "consistently liberal" say the same.[17] We know we are *siloing* when we are unable to relax and relate with people who don't share our convictions.

I sometimes wonder if just for kicks and giggles, Jesus paired up Simon the Zealot (one committed to overthrowing foreign oppressors) and Levi the tax collector (one who collaborated with the foreign regime to gain wealth) when He sent the disciples out two by two. We tend to be drawn to those who are most like us. This seems so natural, but is it true to the movement that Jesus started? Barna research has exposed that "Christians are even more likely not to have friends who are different from them, especially when it comes to religious beliefs (91% mostly similar), ethnicity (88%), and political views (86%)."[18]

These silos we live in create a void, and the void is violent on the growth of love in a Jesus follower. Attack ads, ad-hominem arguments, and excessive claims about each other's impact on America's future have become staple elements of beating back our enemies. The void is fortified by this type of hostile rhetoric about "them," "they," "it." And yet, our fundamental identity is those created and beloved by God—this is the more accurate label Jesus places on us. The mystery seems to be that my enemy shares the same glory that I share in—we are both made in the glorious image of God.

CROSSING THE VOID

There are extraordinary stories of people crossing the void to practice affection toward enemies. They are not the most popular of stories to tell because they don't fit our side-taking, polarizing times. Daryl Davis has lived into enemy-love for thirty years. His home is filled with memories of his relational work spending time with the Ku Klux Klan.[19] Daryl is a descendant of slaves and chose to cross the divide to win over the hearts of those within the white supremacist organization. He knows that deep within the soul of the KKK is a fear that is purely focused on his elimination. Yet this does not deter Daryl; it has actually compelled him to pursue ongoing conversation with Grand Dragons and Imperial Wizards. Sometimes he is the first African American they have ever talked to. Hope, not hate, percolates within Daryl after thirty years of meeting with enemies.[20] You'd think his hopeful outlook is delusional if not for a peek into his bedroom closet.

The shocking symbols of transformation: KKK robes from those who have left behind the Klan are spilling out. Every time he inspires a white man to quit the Ku Klux Klan, they surrender their garb to him. It is a powerful sign of the fruitfulness of Daryl's love-work. His work is not marked by tossing insults or even winning verbal shouting matches but by relational presence with them, sitting with them, eating with them, and showing them a bit of affection.

Daryl Davis reaches out to Billy Snuffer, extending his hand. Billy is a proponent of the Confederate South who thinks the mixing of races is horrible for the country.[21] These small exchanges seem inconsequential, but they have world-altering significance. Daryl has mastered the art of listening: make eye contact, sit still, ask questions, don't interrupt, stay curious. For change to happen, Daryl believes you must move beyond side-taking and move toward affection, even in the face of something as vile as white supremacy. He showed up at court to be with Billy. Billy had fired a gun into the air near a school in Charlottesville during a rally against taking down a Confederate monument. The judge was going to sentence him harshly, but Daryl had an out-of-the-box idea he proposed to the judge that Snuffer meet with him for a regular conversation to hear about the people he sees as inferior.[22]

Daryl often tries to explain his work, but it is repeatedly met with repulsion from both sides. He tells how he reaches for common ground: how he sits, listens, and extends kindness. But this type of enemy-love angers the polarized human heart. He's been officially derided by members of the NAACP and been spat on by members from Unite the Right. Daryl embodies Martin Luther King Jr.'s profound words to both the left and the right: "I am convinced that men hate each other because they fear each other. They fear each other because that don't know each other and they don't know each other because they don't communicate with each other, and they don't communicate with each other because they are separated from each other."[23]

THE ICK FACTOR

When I engage with this story I wonder what it feels like for Daryl Davis to sit with a KKK member, to sense the grotesque hate oozing from his enemies' pores; to know that Billy is part of a lineage of hooded men who strung up human beings on lynching trees. Something happens in our five senses that repels us when we are with our enemies. Part of the fence we erect between us is the ick factor; we feel in some way that to be with them is to get their sin on us.

The reluctant prophet Jonah does not want to blend with the enemy or be contaminated by their evil. I don't blame him. Who wants to sit down with an Assyrian warlord who has dried blood on his hands from killing families? God's love for the Assyrians felt loathsome. The love between the Samaritan and the neighbor on the road felt loathsome. On some level, being near our enemies, being with them, feels like we are getting their stink on us.[24]

We have created monsters in our minds because of hurt and the void that exists between us. Since the Enemy pitted Adam against Eve, and Adam and Eve against God, we have hopelessly needed a healing path beyond our polarizing fear. The enemy-love of God breaks up, like a sledgehammer, the walls our fears build. Jesus is bringing bold, blazing clarity to the kind of love He wants to usher into the world. We are invited into a deepening sense of awe for the wonder of humans, even those who feel like monsters. Who are the monsters in your life? Who is the neighbor you're avoiding? Will you respond to Jesus' invitation to love your enemies? Will you take the path beyond Attacking or Avoiding into Affection?

Reflection Questions

1. What part of the passage on loving enemies is most scandalous to you?

2. What part of affection for monsters brings you some conflict or clarity in your own life?

3. What step can you take to close the void between you and others in the "them" category?

Chapter 5

WHEN LOVE COMES TO TOWN

The search for truth is not an effort to apprehend facts but rather the faithful work to truly see people.
◆ ESTHER MEEKS

I wish putting on affection for your enemies was as simple as putting on a new pair of socks fresh out of the dryer— clean, easy, warm. Love for those we dislike, those we fear, is more than niceties and well wishes. God's invitation to Jonah is beyond words. Jonah must go to the city gates, and ask if he can come in. Love is full-bodied with all of our senses. Love must come to town.

PAST OUR OPINIONS

We might be proud of our well-informed opinions about those who feel like enemies. It's quite trendy, in some circles, to heap scorn on uninformed conservatives and in other spheres to tear apart elitist progressives. Jesus followers must transcend these social ghettos of self-righteousness. If we believe that all of us, even our enemies, are created in the image of God, then we must behold it. Only in the real journey, through the void, can enemy-love become true and tangible. This is what makes the church unique in a world of conflict.

Enemy-love calls us into an utterly peculiar approach— to go ourselves, bearing gifts of peace, of blessing, moving from the center of our convictions to the edge of our comfort zones.[1] But be warned, this full-bodied kind of love will collide with our current ideas on how we think we know people.

THE INFORMATION GOLD RUSH

Over the last couple of decades, something slightly ominous arrived. The phenomenon started back in the '90s with chat rooms and heated up with the slow burn of personal blogs in the 2000s, taking its time to come to full, heaving, undulating boil to what we have now: Expert Delusion.[2] Expert Delusion is the misguided belief that you can be an expert because you have access to information. I'm an expert on gardening because I've read multiple blog articles; I'm an expert on mental health because I've listened to multiple podcasts; I'm an expert on the incarceration system because I've read multiple Twitter threads. At times I'm lured into the lie that I can be an expert on something because I've acquired information on a specific matter—low-carb eating, city planning, constitutional law, etc. Peter Senge unpacks our fixation on becoming experts: "We secure strength in our social worlds when we are convinced we have more accumulated information in our head than anyone else."[3]

The direct impact of this information-binging is that it erodes our ability to enter into the experience of another. It tricks our egos into believing that we already *know* because we are *informed*—it gives us bloated brains (Matt. 23:23). We love information like Kim Jong-un loves to line up his tanks and soldiers in the streets—it provides our egos a sense of conquest and control.

BLOATED BRAINS

The Information Gold Rush we live in collides with our current cultural beliefs in how we "know" things. René Descartes gave us the slogan "I think therefore I am."[4] Descartes, a mathematician, attempted to make all knowledge as certain as he perceived math equations. Descartes defined the self as "Thinker."[5] In the act of "knowing" we tend to picture information, facts, statements, and proofs. Knowledge in our time is factoids. The church gained its convictions about how to hold on to truth from Descartes.

In my early twenties I was fanatical about absolute truth. Which in those days meant facts about reality, not presence *with* others. Truth had little to

We think we can know things about people without dwelling with people. Being right, without loving well, is not right.

do with the relational journey and everything do with information through reading. Blame it on Descartes, we think we can know things about people without dwelling with people.

Being right, without loving well, is not right. If we think knowledge is information, then obviously it's readily available in gargantuan amounts, delivered instantly via the internet, cable news, and your favorite podcast. You can merely let Fox News, CNN, or NPR tell you about large swaths of people:

Black people are _____.

Evangelicals are _____.

Immigrants are _____.

Republicans are _____.

Democrats are _____.

We are being shaped to believe emotionally, psychologically, and relationally that knowledge is the passive consumption of information. We don't know each other, even though we are convinced we do—no wonder we have so many perceived enemies. The way we conceive of truth is essentially impersonal. We fill in the blanks and call them facts about each other.

Recently I was enjoying a meal with some friends when the conversation devolved into talking about another person in a way unflattering to their reputation. In a moment of reckless boldness, I asked, "How do we know these things? Have we spent time with them? Have we asked them?" Hint: that's how you become a party-pooper. The conversation screeched to a halt, and we all hemmed and hawed at realizing our observations were from a place of detachment and hearsay. Now, this type of opinion-creation is an American pastime, but this approach to "knowing" someone is violent to the critical quality that makes us human.

THE DEATH OF EMPATHY

Most cool technological innovations have unintended consequences. We are growing numb to each other.[6] Empathy—the ability to share someone else's feelings—is perhaps the most crucial trait humans can demonstrate. It distinguishes us from the animal kingdom. It allows us to love, learn, communicate, and cooperate in life-giving ways.[7]

I remember the first time one of my close buddies told me that he was attracted to other guys. At that exact moment, my first rumbling impulse was to take a big step back. Why? There is a simple reason—I am not attracted to men. I have never once entertained the thought. I cannot relate—everything in my body, my mind, my chemicals are drawn to the opposite sex. This is not a moral statement; it is a statement of affinity. We are on the other side of the world when it comes to our attractions. Empathy is needed for such sensitive moments when we suddenly find ourselves very different, unable to see what we have in common.

Without empathy, we are forced to cluster and huddle with people who are just like us. The moment we interact with someone we are sniffing out, like bloodhounds, what our differences might be. Too often the moment we feel the prickliness of contrast, a subconscious antagonism swells within, and our guard goes back up.

As informed as we think we are, most of us inhabit information silos of broadcast, print, website and social media, where our own preferences repeat in echo chambers of increasingly hostile and narrow thought.[8] These media outlets not

Our time-saving devices are depleting our tolerance for the relational process.

only damage empathy but move the needle of our ideas and language to extremes. Social media is only exacerbating what is already natural—we like information; it provides us with the convenience to fear each other from a distance. Our time-saving devices are depleting our tolerance for the relational process.

If there is a personality trait that makes the story of God wildly unique, it is empathy. This is essential to understanding the work of Christ in the world.

THE RELATER GOD

Empathy from the vantage point of religion was considered an impossibility in the Greco-Roman world of Jesus' day.[9] Pagan religion believed the gods would occasionally come to the aid of human beings, but the gods could not empathize with us. In the ancient Greek work *The Iliad*, Homer describes the gap between humans and gods: "Such is the way the gods spun life for unfortunate mortals, that we live in unhappiness, but the gods themselves do not understand our sorrows."[10] Additionally, Aristotle criticizes Plato's suggestion that humans should look to God as an example for human conduct for the simple reason that the gods are far removed from human life.

Enter Jesus.

God in Christ modeled for us the *Self as Relater*, not the *Self as Thinker*. Whatever we think we know is merely an opinion, not a full knowing. At its heart, *knowing* is about the relational learning process.[11] This is the path that enemy-love must walk.

The healing we need in the world will not come through the disseminating of information; it will come through the risk of interpersonal presence. God did not send an updated version of the Ten Commandments 2.0. Instead, God came in a physical, vulnerable, wound-able body. The truth of Christ is not a mere proposition; it is a "personed" event.[12] God comes to town; God walks into the room. The incarnation of Christ is God's interpersonal presence. Jesus was a "manger wetter," as the poet Stephen Mahan states. This is not sacrilegious; this is

The healing we need in the world will not come through the disseminating of information; it will come through the risk of interpersonal presence.

sacred. God experienced the full extent of human flesh, even the harrowing parts. Jesus is God, and feels the human experience.

The author of Hebrews presents Jesus as the high priest who "understands our weaknesses" (Heb. 4:15 NLT). In this text, *understanding* and *experience* are directly linked to the way God relates with us. God's empathetic posture was not a strategy; it is the way God is because God is love. Beyond our wildest imaginations, God turns out to be empathetic. Jesus has firsthand experience of our life, using all the senses of taste, sight, touch, smell, and sound.

Back to Hebrews, the verse immediately following illustrates the result of empathy: "Let us then with confidence draw near to the throne of grace" (Heb. 4:16 ESV). Humans, you and I, can now draw closer to the divine. That is to say, the result of Christ's empathy is feeling secure and safe coming nearer to God. Empathy is a link; it creates a connection between people that did not exist prior.

The self-emptying love of Jesus creates these connections. Without this empathetic work, we would not want to come nearer to God. Every Old Testament prophet is frightened by God's presence, but when Jesus arrives with human skin, the full revelation of God, sinners, outcast, gluttons, drunkards, even the rich long to get close. Because of Jesus we no longer need to operate in a spirit of fear. This is the power of empathy—finally someone sees me and understands me!

FACTS DON'T CHANGE MINDS

The human mind desires something else even more than facts and information. It is a fundamental human tendency that none of us are exempt from. The scenario typically goes like this: Someone says or does something that we believe is outright wrong, highly ignorant, or clearly sinful. We respond with a forceful argument, some persuasive speech, or even verbal aggression, believing this will change someone's mind. But nothing ever changes, does it? This is because our brains don't respond well to these tactics.

Our brain is continuously protecting our sense of identity. Our identity is a stew of who we think we are and how we want others to see us. When foreign facts are brought to us, our brains naturally defend and deflect—especially if that new information highlights a flaw in our identity. The same part of the brain that processes physical danger is activated.[13] This is why people often react so aggressively to facts that imply that they might be wrong. The very act of lobbing new information at each other triggers our primal instincts.

Just the other day while in the grocery store, waiting in the checkout line as our two-year-old attempted to pull everything off the shelf, my wife noticed that the person ahead of us had placed an expired container of oatmeal on the conveyor belt. "Excuse me," my wife said, "I just noticed that your oatmeal expired; wasn't sure if you had noticed." The woman responded with some heat: "Who asked you? Mind your own business." My wife apologized for trying to help. Ironically, the woman ended up telling the cashier she didn't want to purchase the oatmeal after all. We naturally repel information that might possibly indict us or inform us of something unflattering.

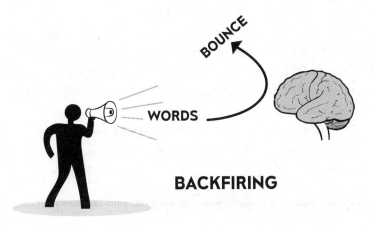

BACKFIRING

Some neurologists have called this the backfiring effect.[14] When information is presented to us that is in opposition to the current truths we hold, we don't often change our minds; we immediately deflect and dig down even harder into our original stance.

In 2006, the University of Michigan and Georgia State University created fake newspaper articles about polarizing political issues.[15] The reports were written in a way that would confirm a widespread misconception. They gathered two groups of thirty people to read them in a room. One group received a fake article, was given time to read it, and then handed a true article that corrected the first. For instance, one suggested the United States had found weapons of mass destruction in Iraq. The next article said the US never found them, which was the truth. Those who already supported the war agreed with the first article and dismissed the second article as false. After reading that there were no WMDs found in Iraq, they reported being even more convinced of their original belief in WMDs in Iraq.[16] Even after the evidence "when beliefs have been totally refuted, people fail to make appropriate revisions in those beliefs," the researchers noted.

New facts, new evidence is not the best way to change our beliefs. I know, it's a bummer. Providing people with accurate information doesn't seem to help. Attacking someone with facts is like fighting a grease fire with water; it seems like it should work but just makes the fire worse.

Convincing someone to change their mind is really the process of convincing them that you really care about them. Perhaps it is not *difference* but *distance* that breeds hostility and hate. As interpersonal presence increases, so does understanding. I am reminded of Abraham Lincoln's quote, "I don't like that man. I must get to know him better." If you want someone who you are polarized against to consider an error in their thinking, first seek tactics that help them see you as *more* human. Despite what you see on every cable news station, it is highly unlikely that the forceful exchange of facts will open our receptivity pores. As Jesus followers, we need to do empathetic work for truer *knowing* between us. We now see that to know something is to have a living relationship with it—an engagement one enters into with attentiveness, care, and affection. This involves our whole selves, not just our mouths and opinions. Interpersonal presence is far richer and more robust than lazy fact-finding.

DISCOVERING EMPATHY

Jon Godfrey is a gun advocate, having quite a few at his upstate New York home. Before he retired, he was in law enforcement and was active in the military. He is an avid hunter and would not hesitate to fend off an intruder with a gun if need be. Jon has become friends with Peter Lotto. Peter has no guns in his Syracuse home. He's retired and adjunct teaches history at several local colleges. Peter sought out Jon, who was part of a pro-gun Syracuse group. He was curious what made Jon tick, not understanding why anyone would ever need to own an AR-15.

Obviously, Jon and Peter are on opposing sides of an exceptionally heated debate.[17] This friendship built by Jon and Peter is unique. Believe it or not, they like each other, and have developed an important connection since meeting in a coffee shop over a year ago. Though they are supposed to be polarized against each other, they moved beyond the outrage of social media to meet face-to-face to explore their disagreements.

The first time they met, they expected to be enemies. While the topic of their conversation revolved around gun control, they spent time talking about their lives, their experiences, and their flaws. What they discovered was how much they had in common and specifically their worry about how unsafe the world has become.[18]

They've learned to "know" each other as people, not as "opinions." Peter shared that they had to learn to discuss the major things they disagree on without demonizing each other. Both affirmed that "listening and asking questions in a way that is curious, not accusing" is the secret. In the process, there was a moment of realization that they were not as far away from each other as previously thought; they began to grow in empathy, and along the way they rubbed off on each other. They both confess to having the hard edges of their opinions softened and even changed because of their conversations.

The vast majority of our disdain and disgust for each other is tossed over our fences of separation—Us vs. Them.[19] Peter and Jon, without knowing it, are a model for the church in what the gospel looks like in the real world. It disrupts the control polarization presses upon us, moves toward another, past fears, like Jesus, seeking an empathetic presence.

PASSING ON PRESENCE

Revisiting Jonah, it was not his words that wooed the Assyrian tyrant king to repentance and to change his ways. The unexpected power is found in his *going* there. His actual physical presence spoke volumes—he went vulnerable. The Assyrians had no way to comprehend this act. It is dumbfounding when a perceived enemy comes susceptible and open. All of the rage, all of the fire, all of the violence ceases, even for a minute, to consider who is before them.[20] The prophetic act of a man who offers his neck to his enemies disrupts an entire empire. Jonah's physical revelation of God's affection points forward to the incarnation of God in Jesus. We must be convinced of the good news of Jesus coming to us, in the flesh, teaching us what love looks like. From that place we are assured: we pass on presence before we pass on information.

My wife and I experienced this on a deeply human level a year ago. We brought into our home a ten-day-old baby who was addicted to cocaine and had alcohol in his little system. Babies are made to be cared for, touched, and engulfed in support. But our foster child needed a more intense presence than

I was ready for. For thirty days, his body shook violently in his withdrawals. Sleep was so excruciating for him. I remember dark nights as he suffered. We could not touch him gently; it freaked his nervous system out. He needed to be squeezed hard, so hard that I thought I must be hurting him. I would clench him tightly to my chest for hours as his body would calm down and eventually relax in the safety of my arms. We passed on presence, and it helped him heal. His first knowledge was the knowledge of the interpersonal.

We are no longer infants, but presence is everyone's love language. The further away we get from a real-time relationship in comprehending those unlike us, or those perceived to be our enemies, the more distorted and demonic we get in our pronouncements. Love presumes that our enemies are worth getting to know.

LOVE MUST DESCEND

To reach the summit of moving past our fears, in affectionate love, we must first descend. A few years back I was climbing a mountain with one of my friends, Chris. We were scaling Whiteface Mountain in the Adirondacks in upstate New York. The elevation is 4,865. We had been climbing all day after starting at 6 a.m. I'm a rookie climber, but Chris was not; he had climbed this mountain before. Almost to the summit after a long, exhausting, exhilarating day, we could see the end in sight. We rested at a little shelf created by some rocks. We drank our Gatorade and nibbled on our granola bars. From my vantage point, it looked like we only had about fifteen minutes left of climbing.

Chris interrupted my premature celebration and said, "We aren't going to climb straight up, we have to go down first." We had to spelunk a cave through the mountain to climb up to the summit from the other side. We would have to leave our gear at the mouth of the cave because we wouldn't be able to make it through carrying our equipment. The cave was pitch-black, cold, and filled with bats and bugs. This seemed bizarre to me, even a bit of a time waster. Descending into the cave would add almost another two hours of climbing. Chris declared something that has lodged in me ever since: "Dan, climbing is not a straight line to the top, sometimes you have to go down in order to go up." We can reach the apex of revelation that God is love, but to go higher up that holy mountain, we must enter into the process downward to love our enemies. Jonah experienced this. His journey of transformation, into perfect love, would take him into the dark, cold cave of the belly of the fish.

We often want a spirituality of success without the holiness of descent. We want to find a way to love that only requires a minuscule sacrifice from us. Love in our time has become convoluted by feeling good about ourselves, affirmation of our desires, and an overall positive vibe. So we have an allergic reaction to a love that induces discomfort within. Naturally, this is why we gravitate toward people like us and away from people unlike us. As we will see in Jesus, there is no possibility, no power, no phenomenon of love without costly work. This polarization-busting, bridge-building, enemy-befriending love will require us to wrestle with the way of love; we will feel these feels that Jonah felt: "Thou hadst cast me into the deep, in the midst of the seas; and the floods compassed me about: all thy billows and thy waves passed over me" (Jonah 2:3 KJV). Loving others, especially those unlike us, can overwhelm us with the waves of emotions—fear, anger, and even hatred. Personally, I have never been able to skip this stage, the place of descending the floorboards of my soul to battle with

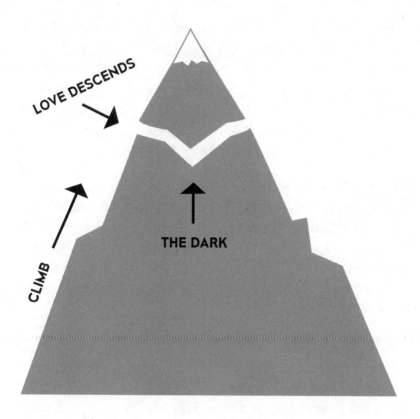

the hot hatred gurgling below. To move toward our perceived monsters, we must collide with ourselves.

The belly of the aquatic monster is a place of darkness, of internal suffering. It is ironic that to love those we perceive as monsters, we first have to face our own monsters. Jonah is dramatically plunged into a murky ocean sitting in a stew of gross guts. That dark belly symbolizes the place where we have it out with ourselves and with God. Being swallowed by a fish was a gift sent to

Being swallowed by a fish was a gift sent to Jonah to loosen and unhinge his grip on enemy-hatred.

131

Jonah to loosen and unhinge his grip on enemy-hatred. Jonah literally calls the belly of the beast "Sheol" (Jonah 2:2 NKJV). It feels like hell to face the fact that something must die if we are to move toward love. Something must be let go, must be emptied out of us.

LOVE THAT SELF EMPTIES

In 1958, C. S. Lewis shared on a radio show the nature of four distinct loves in the Bible. He thought these loves also resonated with our human experience. Eventually, he wrote a book called *The Four Loves* that developed this out. I see the emotional muscle of affection in all these distinct kinds of loves. But with each love, the work of *affection* moves from being easy to a bit more difficult.

The first love is *storge*, which is family love. A love offered through the fondness of familiarity. An example is the natural love of a parent for their child. In this love, it's probably the most natural to feel *affection*.

The second love is *phileo*. This love is between friends where we share common values, interests, or activities.[21] This love is often talked about between brothers and sisters and Christ in the letters of Paul. Here we don't always naturally feel *affection*, but it does grow between us the more we feel belonging.

The third love is *eros*. This is love in the sense of "being in love." This is a romantic love that draws us toward another to enjoy them emotionally, mentally, spiritually, and physically. Here we find affection so much more natural, although it can be stilted and stifled when our marriages are unhealthy.

The fourth love is *agape* love. This love is ascribed to God. It is a love that cares for us no matter the circumstances. This *agape* love is what flows from the Trinity. The Father, Son, and Spirit set Their affections upon us.

I sense the kind of love we need to be present with our enemies includes *agape* love but goes beyond it and is uniquely offered to us in the visible life of Jesus. This love is the only thing strong enough to transform our fears, draw us toward our enemies. It is revealed in the classic letter to the Christian community in Philippi:

> So if there is any encouragement in Christ. . . . Let each of you look not only to his own interests, but also to the interests of others. Have this mind among yourselves, which is yours in Christ Jesus, who, though he was in the form of God, did not count equality with God a thing to be grasped, but emptied himself, by taking the form of a servant, being born in the likeness of men. (Phil. 2:1, 4–7 ESV)

This is one of the oldest hymns sung in the early Christian community; in a vivid way the hymn shows how Jesus brought an unusual love to people walled off from Him. At the center is the word *kénōsis*, which is translated "emptied." It is not an emptying forced upon Him, but in this case, it's an intentional, chosen, self-emptying. The meaning of "emptied" suggests a voluntary humbling that Jesus takes to be present with His human creation, even those who oppose Him. This word kenosis appears five times in the New Testament to describe the love-journey of Jesus.

For Paul, kenosis is not just one of many moral attitudes, but a decisive one that claimed the entire physical pilgrimage of love. Kenosis is metaphysical—the only path for crossing the divides we face. Jesus descended into the cave. Indeed Jesus is a person, but at the same time, Jesus is a process to enter into.[22] Jesus is the Son of God, but He is also "the way"—the way of kenosis. There are no shortcuts around it if we desire to grow in our capacity to love.

It has become increasingly more apparent to me that there is no chance for any deep transformation into perfect love without descent, without dying. When we look at the openness in Christ that many recognized, drew people toward Him like a magnet, and freed Him to move toward them—what was it? Paul marries it to Christ's kenosis. Kenosis gives space for others to be who they are, near us, without judgment. We make space for the expression of their existence in our life. His kenosis, the self-emptying of His glory, made space for the glutton, the drunkard, the prostitute, the tax collector, the betrayer to be with Him, and for Him to be with them. He could enjoy their presence as they enjoyed His. Kenosis creates space for people to belong.

We are now given the same commission as Jesus. Without kenosis, I cannot, I probably will not, make space to be still, listen, make eye contact, and enjoy the presence of someone whose moral choices I loathe. Without kenosis, my opinions, my preferences, my way of life must be centered, highlighted, respected. We can now move out into the world: "In your relationships with one another, have the same mindset as Christ Jesus" (Phil. 2:5). When we empty ourselves, we create a space to step toward others we are polarized against; our conservative neighbor, our progressive neighbor, our immigrant neighbor, our gay

> **Kenosis gives space for others to be who they are, near us, without judgment. It creates space for people to belong.**

barista, our Trump-voting grandpa, our socialist-championing grad student.

THE IRRITATION OF LOVE

Our struggle is often not whether we agree with the theology of "enemy-love" nearly as much as it is about our over-defended emotions. Intellectually, we know the point of the parable of the Good Samaritan, but we don't like the way it feels.[23] Our emotional reactions to people are so rapid that they override every Sunday school lesson we've ever heard about loving our enemies. Thus, the war between fear and love is waged in those in instantaneous flashes of contempt, irritation, anger, or disgust we feel toward others.[24] Those feelings flood our brains, light up our amygdala, and hijack our good theology before we even have time to imagine a more affectionate way. We must not skate over the surface of our lives—we must explore what's controlling us.

Although the objects of our fears are often external, the real source of our fear is internal. The monster is one's self—at least some aspects of the self. The work of love wages war within, when we are confronted with our true feelings. This is what our friend Jonah faced in the guts of that big fish. In the dark, in the deep, we toss and turn with how awesome and how awful God's enemy-love feels to us.[25] God's tender kindness toward enemies genuinely irritates us. We feel repelled by love like this. We must face ourselves honestly, that we, like Jonah, don't really want Nineveh to be touched by God.

When I have an impulse to love someone unlike me, something rises up inside me, a bile of annoyance, of indifference—a whole range of self-preoccupied emotions that seek to shut down the action of love. It scorches my throat and burns hot in my soul. Part of this self-emptying journey is acknowledging I want to be right more than I want to connect. This truth I've writhed with—I don't want to be near my enemies. They deserve the worst, and marinating on this "worst" falling upon their heads brings me a twisted pleasure. Conversing with my enemies feels like validating them—blasting them with verbal grenades would be so much more cathartic.

This is the lava boiling in the volcano of my soul. We must face our own monster within before we can move toward the monsters in our life with affection. This is not a moping drudgery driven by self-loathing or self-pity. It's not a work of self-hatred either. It's a clear-eyed entry into what controls us, what holds us hostage to the way of fear. The entry point into enemy-love is a power-surrender, a self-emptying process that brings healing to us so that we might extend that healing to others.

ULTIMATE KENOSIS

The cross is the ultimate kenosis: Christ was emptied to the point of death. Orthodox priest Kallistos Ware states so beautifully:

> The victory of his suffering love upon the Cross does not merely set me an example, showing me what I myself may imitate. It is that but also much more than that, his suffering love has a transforming effect on my own heart and will, releasing me from bondage, healing me, rendering it possible for me to love in a way that would be beyond my own willpower, had I not first been loved by him. Because in love he has identified with me, brought his victory to my body. And so Christ's death upon the Cross is truly a life-creating death.[26]

The cross cannot and should not be robbed of the scandal that it is. When we look at the cross, do we begin to comprehend God's revelation of *affection* toward us"? We must breathe it into our lives and breathe it out. Be still. Behold it. Dwell on it. Let it disrupt you. Jesus is punched, kicked, spit on, mocked, humiliated, and He responds with the most tender words imaginable: "Father, forgive them, for they do not know what they are doing" (Luke 23:34). This is the gospel! Rather than killing His enemies He dies for them instead—arms outstretched welcoming those who hurled insults at Him.[27]

When Jesus' enemies sought to crush Him, He did not cook up a scheme to crush them back. I am undone by this. I can hardly restrain from a snarky response when someone insults me, but here Jesus restrains Himself from calling legions of angels to destroy those who smash a crown of thorns onto His head. To put it into the language of the apostle Paul, "while we were still sinners, Christ died for us" (Rom. 5:8). The cross is the event by which God's enemy-love is most shockingly displayed. This is kenosis—God's full willingness to pour out love before the faces of His enemies!

Instead of fighting people, He fought Satan, stripping him of dominating power (Col. 2:15). Our war is not with flesh and blood; it is not with each other. That is Satan's diversion tactic in polarizing us. The work of the cross dethroned an illegitimate, fear-based ruler and reinstated a loving, legitimate one. Fear and love went to war on the cross, and love triumphed. We are now empowered to love, a kenotic-love, setting aside parts of ourselves for the sake of making space to connect with others unlike us. We can give ourselves over to this wild love. This is a work of the Spirit, making Christ's spirit ours, and His love ours. We may feel some resistance within, but we

We should not take kenosis as a sign of weakness because it is actually a demonstration of bravery.

know that it is the path pioneered for us in Jesus.

In our polarized world, there is only imagination for winners and losers, so to contemporary competitive minds this might look defeatist. The apostle Paul concedes that this kind of enemy-love looks like "foolishness" but rather it is the wisdom of God (1 Cor. 1:18, 24). A new picture for "winning" is being released into the world through kenosis. We should not take kenosis as a sign of weakness because it is actually a demonstration of bravery. Kenosis is the paradoxical form of power that God uses to disrupt the world.

BIRTHING A NEW LOVE

We are invited to follow Jesus' footsteps to Calvary, to take up our cross, whether it's our fear, our dread, our hatred, our cowardice, or our need for security, and surrender it all. Only after we have died to the enemy-hatred that we hold white-knuckled can we be raised up to new life—gaining access to the resurrection power of God. The moment of kenosis is the moment we give healing a chance to see daylight.

Birth is a beautiful and bloody process—there's no way around it. I almost passed out at our first son's birth. The volume of blood was too much for me to handle. An hour later when I was holding a pink-skinned little human that fit into my two palms, I could not believe that from that bloody mess came this beautiful miracle. There is a bizarre detail in the text of Jonah's story. The Hebrew for "great fish" switches from the masculine to the feminine when Jonah is spit up onto dry land. Jonah was being reborn into perfect love. Becoming new. Out of the mess, trial, and darkness came renewal—new life, new possibilities.

Sometimes kenosis feels like cleaning out a cluttered garage. First, we have to admit that we've allowed a lot of junk to store up. We come to terms with how much anger and offense we've hoarded inside. So, we get oversized garbage bags, work gloves, and a broom and begin the scrubbing and scraping process. I've wrestled in the dark with the torment of loving enemies, but from this dark place, something holy begins to sprout inside me, as if the Spirit is decluttering my soul. Such realities don't so much give us new beliefs, per se—they give us new energy for the truth. I've always believed in enemy-love, I just needed to be converted to its practice. When the divine touches us, we can show affection to the perceived monster's in our life. Resurrection has filled my bones and compelled me to go and love Nineveh. Who is the Nineveh in your life?

Reflection Questions

1. What part of "knowing through relational presence" is interesting to you? Why?

2. What part of "kenosis to love enemies" brings you some conflict or clarity in your life?

3. What step can you take to face the monster within yourself?

Chapter 6

BREAKING OPEN SPACE

Judging others makes us blind, whereas love is illuminating. By judging others we blind ourselves to our own evil and to the grace which others are just as entitled to as we are. ◆ DIETRICH BONHOEFFER

The orange extension cord in my basement is alive. I have no idea how it got this way. I'm sure that I wrapped it up loosely in a reasonably organized fashion, but every time I go to use it, it is somehow wound up, tangled in a massive, maddening maze of knots. I've lost my temper too many times on that extension cord. If you try to pull on the opposite ends to unwind it, it only binds into an expletive-inducing tightness. It's like a cruel game.

To move beyond our fears, beyond our polarization, we

cannot just pull on "our side" with the power of our arguments, our proofs that we're in the right, on the side of righteousness, or on the side of justice. It only tightens the knots. You've felt it, I've felt it—we are getting nowhere. There is no oxygen to breathe; even a compliment would be interpreted as a jab. This is what happens when antagonism has wound us tight.

CAUGHT IN ANTAGONISM

Antagonism moves beyond the event that offended us and constricts our interpretations of each other, so we only see caricatures—all Republicans support white supremacists, or all Democrats support sexual immorality. This polarized predicament gives us two options to either wholeheartedly agree or vehemently disagree, get behind it or resist it. Our judgments get locked in and pick up their own energy. There is where we find ourselves, in the inertia of antagonism, justifying our exaggerations, believing the worst about each other. This is what antagonism does— thrusts us into one ditch or the other, stuck like a car spinning its wheels in a snow bank. You're not going anywhere, no movement, no matter how hard you stomp on the gas.

Have you felt this in your family?

Have you felt this in your church?

I know what it's like to be consumed and controlled by antagonism. I know what it's like to dig my heels in, to just pull harder, to stroke my inner ego with words like "I'm the one in the right." I hold a little vigil in my mind, waiting for the other person to validate every feeling I've ever had about them as irrefutable truth. This is where the work of love should scandalize us, where the way of Jesus should disrupt our entrenched standoffs.

Twenty years ago, my wife and I had our first big fight. Somewhere in the middle of yelling at each other, I realized she was partially right—a little hiccup in my argument was exposed. At that point, I feared that if I gave a few inches then she would take a mile. My ego refused to budge; it vied for supreme protection. I was too prideful to concede even one point. The majority of our antagonism concerns us with the security of our ego. My wife and I have since developed much healthier habits when we disagree, but that moment is suspended in my mind: when I could have given an inch, I would not give it.

We know what this looks like in our highly partisan times. We see the antagonism, the virtual war that breaks out on social media. There is a distorted delight in mocking our political enemies. This antagonism keeps our democracy energized, gives political pundits a job, and creates our two-party system. We are no longer engaging real people. We are fighting shadow monsters, a perceived understanding of each other.

An essential step toward unwinding the antagonism is not to *pull* harder. This only entrenches our current hostility. We don't need better arguments, well-crafted zingers, or a megaphone to yell louder through—we need creative disruption. We must break open space to see each other anew, to make space for connection, to make room for presence. Someone, anyone must go first.

JESUS THE CREATIVE DISRUPTER

Jesus is continuously faced with the heat of antagonism. In John 8:1–11 (NLT) we get a glimpse of His creative disruption:

Jesus returned to the Mount of Olives, but early the next morning he was back again at the Temple. A crowd soon gathered, and he sat down and taught them. As he was speaking, the teachers of religious law and the Pharisees brought a woman who had been caught in the act of adultery. They put her in front of the crowd.

"Teacher," they said to Jesus, "this woman was caught in the act of adultery. The law of Moses says to stone her. What do you say?"

They were trying to trap him into saying something they could use against him, but Jesus stooped down and wrote in the dust with his finger. They kept demanding an answer, so he stood up again and said, "All right, but let the one who has never sinned throw the first stone!" Then he stooped down again and wrote in the dust.

When the accusers heard this, they slipped away one by one, beginning with the oldest, until only Jesus was left in the middle of the crowd with the woman. Then Jesus stood up again and said to the woman, "Where are your accusers? Didn't even one of them condemn you?"

"No, Lord," she said.

And Jesus said, "Neither do I. Go and sin no more."

Jesus encounters a mob that is ready to bury an adulterous woman with stones. Notice, they place her before the mob (v. 3). She is no longer a person, she's an object for their anger.[1] Jesus disrupts the mob mentality. If you find yourself joining in with others to heap scorn, mockery, or shame on an individual—whether publicly or privately—God is not with you in those actions. The energy of group hatred romanticizes us and swallows us up.

In the midst of this ferocious crowd, Jesus is asked if this woman should be stoned as the Law of Moses commanded (John 8:5). Did this woman do something wrong? Yes. She broke the law, according to God's law. This woman did what she was accused of. Why is this important to notice? Most of our polarization and antagonism is focused on rights and wrongs. Who is the offender? In this situation, this unnamed woman is the offender. Jesus even confirms this in His later response when He tells her to "go, and sin no more" (John 8:11 KJV). This brings us back to how polarization shapes us to focus *solely* on black and white, right and wrong, either/ or. Our imaginations must graduate beyond the logic of who did something bad. This is hard for us. This ethic governs our entire society.

LAW CULTURE

American culture is thick with the consciousness of Law and Order. The foundations of our society were formed in the courtroom, ever since the first settlers to America brought the criminal justice system of England to our shores. Their system was based on the premise of *mens rea*, translated from Latin is "guilty mind."[2] The "guilty mind" is that people must know they are doing something wrong before they can be found guilty and branded a criminal. So, therefore, the establishment of laws helps people feel guilty for their actions. Without laws to govern daily life, our conscience would not know we are doing wrong. *Mens rea* intrinsically carried a distrust for human conscience and trust for an authoritative system to help us be better humans.

To bring order out of the chaos after the American Revolution, in 1789, the Judiciary Act was established to give authority to the courts of the United States. It was signed into law by President Washington.[3] After the American Revolution eventually came the formation of the US Constitution, which reigned supreme over all people's rights and freedoms. The courts brought clarity to our daily lives. Theodore Roosevelt gave even more momentum to this in the early 1900s by establishing more legal structures: enforcement agencies (such as the FBI), stronger prison sentences, and a juvenile justice system. Roosevelt was convinced a civil society is a legislated society.[4]

Our relationships with each other have been powerfully shaped by what is lawful and what is not. When human relationships break down in our society, we depend on "the law" to sift out the good from the bad. This is our collective mind about how to coexist. Without law, we don't know how to do business with each other, how to live in the neighborhood together, how to cooperate for the common good. When something goes wrong, we carry the illusion that after we find the guilty party, some legislation or policy will prevent the wrong from happening again. Is there anything wrong with law? Well no, and yes. Before you start thinking I'm an anarchist, I'd like to explore how this has fundamentally impacted us, especially followers of Jesus.

SEEING THROUGH LAW

When we are shaped so intensely by "law," it is increasingly tough to see the humanity in each other. Jesus continually collides with the Pharisees over this fundamental visionary shift. The teachers of the Law accuse Jesus of letting the disciples eat food without washing their hands (Matt. 15). Jesus is accused of violating the Sabbath (Luke 6). The list goes on and on as "the Law" was of utmost importance to the Pharisees but secondary to Jesus. Consider the apostle Paul's view of law. On one hand, he believed the law was good (Rom. 7:12). On the other hand, it serves to only increase sin (5:20; 7:5–11). It might seem like Paul was conflicted over the value of law. Rather, he is sharing his own spiritual journey out of law, when he says "who will rescue me from this body that is subject to death?" (7:24).[5] That "who" is Jesus, who set Paul free from the punishing weight of the law. He discovered an entirely new way to live, union with Christ, not union with law. Law culture arises for good, ethical reasons but has serious side effects on our ability to relate with others. We see through law, but it can blind us to something greater.

RELATIONAL CULTURE

Contrast our current US culture with indigenous Native American tribes. Locally, here in Syracuse, we have the joy of the Onondaga Nation bordering our city. I've learned much about how they interact with law and engage in justice. Before the arrival of Englanders to the shores of America, their culture relied upon the oral tradition, and very few aspects of their culture were written down. Consider how being "oral" requires people to actually meet with each other because there are no Constitution, bylaws, or state codes to buffer, to do the work for them. Relationship was the fulcrum for the law. Everything changes when we are required to talk to each other.

The Peace Circle is the traditional way they resolve both criminal and civil issues. This presents a clear contrast to Western courtrooms. The Peace Circle has arisen over generations from each community's culture and collective life experience.

The Peace Circle emphasizes healing over guilt, restoration over punishment, and togetherness over isolation.[6] Stanley L. Nez from the Navajo Nation refers to peacemakers as "healers" instead of judges, and "describes a peacemaking session as a 'ceremony' rather than a hearing or trial." Ultimately, "peacemaking is about relationships," says Barbara A. Smith of the Chickasaw Nation, so, "it becomes . . . a life tool, so that if you have some conflicts . . . you learn how to talk and listen and learn from one another, how to respect whatever the other person is saying, even if you disagree."[7]

I've experienced this myself. Those who feel they've been treated unjustly sit in a circle to introduce themselves and are encouraged to share not only facts (their biographies) but their feelings (their expectations for the coming conversation). A typical peacemaking session begins with a ritual prayer introduced by the moderator. Following the prayer, we all sit in a circle around burning wood, such as cedar, which is the tree of life in their culture. We all receive a piece to throw in the fire, which absorbs the groups' problems, carrying them via smoke into the air, away from the group.

From the outset, it is clear that peacemaking is less rooted in rigid rules and legal concepts and more in the malleable nature of human relationships. I've experienced on a deep level from Onondaga Nations leader Tadodaho Sid Hill that the work of peace is tied to the work of connection.[8] A peacemaking session is less likely to rehash the facts of a conflict or crime and more likely to explore the crime's emotional impact. Anybody can be as angry, as disgusted, as terrified as they want without attacking anybody else. Not that there aren't any boundaries to that, but they get to express the full impact of what they are feeling. The focus here is profound—on *relating* rather than *law*.

IDOL FOOD AND RELATIONSHIP

This reminds me of the way that the apostle Paul engaged a squabble in the Corinthian church. A prohibition is clearly communicated in Acts 15: "You are to abstain from food sacrificed to idols, from blood, from the meat of strangled animals . . ." (v. 29; see also v. 20). Paul forbade Christians from any association with any food overtly connected to idolatry. He understands the confession of one Lord to require loyalty so that even a token gesture to an idol compromises allegiance to Christ.

There were many layers to food sacrificed to idols. Many social engagements were at pagan temples since rooms could be rented out for private functions, like church halls today. Additionally, people did not separate their economic, religious, and social lives in the ancient world, so to eat this food was a visible public participation in Corinth's cultic life.[9]

Christians would quite regularly be offered food that had been sanctified to an idol by a host who was devoted to other gods.[10] They might be able to avoid overt associations with idolatry by not bowing down to shrines, but what were they to do when they were guests at someone's house?

The apostle Paul seems a bit contradictory in his answer. On the one hand, he says consuming idol food was not good, elevated to the sin of immorality (Acts 15:20, 29). But then on the other hand, in 1 Corinthians 8:1–11 he rebukes them for being under-empathic toward "the weak."[11] He gives them permission to munch on food sacrificed to idols: "We are no worse if we do not eat, and no better if we do" (1 Cor. 8:8). Did Paul and the elders in Acts change their mind? Probably not.

Paul chastises the Corinthian Christians not for eating idol food but for knowledge without love: "We know that 'We all possess knowledge.' But knowledge puffs up while love builds up" (1 Cor. 8:1). What is the knowledge Paul is referring to? The knowledge is that eating food sacrificed to idols is a sin. But the apostle Paul is not so much vexed by breaking the law of consuming idol food but by their lack of empathic love for each other.[12] He is essentially appealing to a Relational Culture vs. a Law Culture. Paul does not give a straight answer to the question "Is eating food sacrificed to idols a sin?" but shifts the focus toward Christian love, and in doing so he presents an example of where love and relationship transcend the rightness or wrongness of the act itself. The main concern for Paul is not getting the Corinthians to avoid idolatrous behavior (though that's important) but getting them to preeminently live out the holiness of love: "Let no one seek his own good, but the good of his neighbor" (1 Cor. 10:24 ESV).

FROM LEGALITIES TO LOVE

Our "law culture" may work in some ways, but it does not give us an imagination nor the tools relationship requires. Law may keep us off each other's lawns, but it does not teach us how to love our neighbor. In some ways "law" conditions us to default to legalities instead of conversation. Our law culture has shaped us for one thing—who is right and who is wrong. But this is not the sole priority for Jesus. We are getting a snapshot of how "mercy triumphs over judgment" (James 2:13) when Christ engages the mob—relationship over law. To break open space when we're wound-tight in antagonism, when we're locked into polarization, we must see beyond the categories of right and wrong, no matter how much this irks our instincts. After repeated moments of silence and doodling in the sand, Jesus makes a tongue-in-cheek statement to the angry crowd: "Let any one of you who is without sin be the first to throw a stone at her."

This one-liner gets at the heart of the matter; we like to throw rocks, we like to hurl judgments. We aren't the only ones who struggle with this; Jesus' own disciples did quite frequently. At one point they imply to Jesus that a man was born blind because someone sinned: "Rabbi, who sinned: this man or his parents, causing him to be born blind?" (John 9:2 MSG).

The very question exposes their lens for observing the world and people. They see themselves as *judgers* (as we often do as well). "Why is that man homeless? Does he not want to work?" "Why are that woman's kids out of control? Is she a bad mom?" "Why is that black teenager flunking out of school? Are his parents not at home?" "Why is that person gay? Did his dad not love him?" We ask these type of questions because we're looking to blame. Who did something wrong here? Who's at fault? Heavy within this mob, within the disciples, and within us is a judgmental spirit. Where does this come from?

OVERCOMING JUDGINESS

This desire to be a *judgy* goes back to Genesis 2. There are two trees in the garden of Eden. The Tree of Life is a symbol of God as Provider. This tree is a gift; Adam and Eve are to eat freely from it. Then we have the Tree of the Knowledge of Good and Evil. This tree is a symbol of God as Judge, God as the source of knowledge (DO NOT EAT). As we all know, Adam and Eve become discontent with this arrangement. They want more, more power, more status, they wanted what God had. What did God have?

The Father, Son, and Spirit alone hold the authority to

judge right from wrong. We were never intended to hold that kind of power, to wield judgment from on high.[13] This is not our throne to sit in. Adam and Eve clawed and grabbed for a power reserved for God, and it has proved our undoing ever since. We are not meant to be judges. I know . . . it comes so easily. It comes so easily that it's hard to imagine life without making regular pronouncements about the goodness or badness of people. We have eaten the fruit of the tree and made it a fundamental part of our religious diet.

THE SEPARATOR

The Greek root for the word judgment is *krino*, meaning "to separate." Judgment separates us from certain people. It gives us a false sense of being on higher ground; having power over another that is entirely reserved for God.[14] Scripture uniformly testifies that God alone is Judge and warns us of human judgment's delusional magic. "You hypocrite, first take the plank out of your own eye, and then you will see clearly to remove the speck from your brother's eye" (Matt. 7:5). We cannot handle the power of judgment; we will always see others' sins as much smellier than our own. Can we relate with each other differently? Dietrich Bonhoeffer, in his book *Ethics*, helps us understand that judgmentalism suffers from false seeing. It is a love affair with our own words, expectations, and ideas. You cannot love real and raw people with the judgmental mind, because you'll always try to control them, fix them, or size them up before you give yourself in love to them.

The "judger" inside us feels intolerant with the moral choices others make. You can be a conservative judger or a progressive judger; looking, straining, recording the misdeeds of others. So many of the shifts we make are just moving from one seat of the seesaw to the other and telling ourselves every-thing has changed. We question our old belief system—but don't question the way we carry it. We can carry our beliefs, whether nostalgic conservatism or enlightened progressivism, in the same packaging of harsh judgment and law. Changing people's belief systems is overrated. What changes our lives ultimately will be how we receive and give love. Without waking the human spirit to the presence of love, our law-based guilt maneuvers only produce rigid conformity or passive compliance.

Right after the last presidential election, I had to meet with a fellow who had some major beefs with me. We had never really been close, but he picked up some problems with the fact that I did not endorse a specific candidate in the national election. The day before the meeting, I felt like I was preparing for the SAT, studying every possible answer I might have for his accusations. Holding court in my head, I rehearsed all my defenses—if he says this, I'll say this, if he says that, I'll bring up this, round and round I went. By midday, I was exhausted, and the meeting was still a full twenty-four hours away. When facing an "enemy," I was grasping at leverage for gaining the upper hand—to get control. I confess it did not initially cross my mind to seek relational connection, to look for common ground, to move toward him with affection. There was a bit of self-congratulatory enjoyment in the law-court in my mind, that I may be able to expose his error. But what if we cared more about connecting than judging?

CONNECTION CHANGES EVERYTHING

In the passage about the woman caught in adultery, Jesus is doing something more crucial than casting blame. Perfect love is concerned with something more important than who did what. Love is beyond the *words* said, or *what* was done; it is relentlessly focused on the *way* we are with each other. Love draws us to ask different questions and look for different clues. Connection is at the center of this story. Without relational connection, there is no hope for change, no hope for healing.

We long for connection:

- A discouraged mother comforted by another mother who understands her self-doubt.

- A distraught father warms his son with an embrace that cuts through a hardened heart.

- A younger woman listens deeply to an elderly woman's stories and validates her wisdom.

- A middle-aged man sits on the sidewalk with a homeless young man and affirms his dignity.

- Neighbor comforts neighbor as they share their life regrets over a bonfire.

Nothing, absolutely nothing, can replace the soul's hunger for living, in-person, real-time connection. Without being rooted in it, even disciplined to it, we drift into isolation and verbal criticism of each other. From the first foundations of our world, we were hardwired for connection; it is our divine DNA. We must resist its increasing irrelevance in our technological world by keeping it sacred.

Energy has been placed within us that we are to release toward others in a way that promotes divine connection.[15] Like a doctor pouring healthy blood into an anemic body, God's Spirit pours the energy of Christ into our veins.[16] Our movement toward another is metaphysical. The profound meeting when the truest part of one's soul meets the recesses in another and sees the image of God in another—the good and beautiful. When love passes from one to another, there is a giving and receiving that leaves them both fuller and less terrified of being in the world. Connection disrupts the fear, the antagonisms that twist and turn between us.

We were hardwired for connection; it is our divine DNA. We must resist its increasing irrelevance in our technological world by keeping it sacred.

The Supernatural Connection

The mob rolls in like a thunderstorm with their lightning bolts of judgment. God is not boxed into relating with us by the confines of the "law." He is more attuned to people and their value as image-bearers. To break open space when we are wound tight like an extension cord, we must resist the urge to join the world's terms of polarization. Our ability to debate another into submission is the weakest tool we have at our disposal. We instead enter the world to make space for something new. We must see moments with others, especially our enemies, as opportunities for God's Spirit to awaken us.

The first place I've needed to experience this awakening by the Spirit was in my marriage. I got married young at twenty-one; I was often full of myself, full of needs, full of self-obsessed thoughts, full of unfounded opinions. There's a radio station playing in your head all day, spinning the songs of anxiety about your worth and insecurity about your contribution to the world. Will I be something special, something recognized, something others cannot ignore? Though I loved my wife so desperately, I was *unaware* of how much more I loved myself, and every contour of my wants. The world revolved around me and the way I wanted things. I was a judger—I didn't have any idea.

Tonya and I were visiting my folks from out of town, staying for a week. One afternoon I went for a drive with my dad. He gently asked if we could chat for a minute.

I remember the statement vividly. "Dan, I taught you something that I wish I had never taught you." "Huh, what's that?" I asked, waiting for the punchline. "How to criticize your wife. I criticized every move your mom made when you were kids, and it hurt her." I felt the sting. So I reacted with self-defense. We drove home in silence as I licked my wounds.

I speed walked into the house, looking to get a conversation with my wife ASAP. Rehashing the whole encounter, I looked for some sympathy. Expecting the "I can't believe it" to come spilling out of her mouth, instead she was quiet and was crying. She shared, quivering, that I was continually judging her; I made her feel she could never do anything right. The list of judgments: not driving correctly on the highway, not packing for a day trip perfectly, not communicating with precision, not cooking a meal properly. I had the habit of pointing out everything as either right or wrong. I had a law, a standard I held over her, and it was crushing.

I'm forty-two now, and I'm a recovering judger. My healing from that sickness started twenty years ago. I trace it all back to a moment of connection. My dad inhabited an intimate space. I am grateful he did not accuse, rather inviting me to consider by vulnerably sharing his own faults, his own crimes of judgment. The Spirit entered into that space and turned the lights on in a dark, "judgy" part of my soul.

TUNING INTO CONNECTION

The easiest thing to do at the precise moment Jesus is confronted with the mob's rage is for Him to take a side. As polarization goes, we are often invited to take a side with force, blast out a tweet, unleash a fury of words, and feel the urgency of the moment—it's what polarization does. It is stunning how often Jesus refuses to enter into the terms presented to Him.

But Jesus keys into the Spirit, making room for creative connection in space and time. The connection is disruptive and impedes the raging energy of things: the plans, the agendas, and the habits we find ourselves cemented in.

When love becomes disruptive, it gets at our instinctual core and demands more than a cursory acknowledgment. Jesus did not meet the blunt force of fear with fear. He did not combat law with law. Jesus was liberated by the Father's love to slow down and choose a creative relational approach.

How often are we ready to stone someone with our words, our labels, our arguments? Those who were quite ready to stone the woman suddenly see their "selves" in the absurdity of the moment.[17]

Jesus illustrates that as image-bearers we are all in the same place, we all need God's love, we all sin. There is no hierarchy of sinners, only a healing we all need. This is what my dad communicated when he gently stated, "I taught you something that I wish I never taught you." We should come to our enemies humbly, being human, not being a judge.

Jesus does not throw away orthodoxy; He extends its true intent into the soul of this woman.

The antagonism is broken. One by one the accusers disperse. The woman is left with Jesus, cleared of all the strife and hate. Only after she is released from judgment does Jesus then say, "Neither do I condemn you; go and sin no more" (John 8:11 NKJV). Ironically, once the law-enforcers disbanded, Jesus reasserts the true sense of the law.[18] He does not throw away orthodoxy; He extends its true intent into the soul of this woman. Jesus is faced with the clear, black-and-white command of Scripture, and first chooses mercy. This is shocking when we see it, and when we encounter it in our ordinary lives.

OFFERING CONNECTION IN BATTLE

Recently, a friend of mine shared this story of disruptive connection. In an urban apartment complex in San Antonio, there was a gated tennis court in the complex. The tennis court was kept in pristine condition; its fence was locked and could only be unlocked by members of the apartment complex. Adjacent to the tennis court, but outside the fence was a basketball court where many of the teenagers would play pickup basketball. In the summer heat, between games, the kids would jump the tennis court fence in order to get a drink from the only water fountain on the apartment grounds. This created a significant argument between apartment residents. A faction grew between those who didn't mind teenagers jumping the fence and those who thought it was ruining the tennis court. People took sides, formed two coalitions, and began to say awful things about each other through social media. The apartment Facebook page was a hot mess. The language of fear was everywhere. One person said, "I fear we are telling kids they can't be kids," and another said, "I fear we are telling kids they can be vandals."

Then one sunny afternoon, a creative disruption occurred. Across the street from the apartment complex and the basketball court someone installed, on their own dime, a free drinking fountain in their own front yard and posted a sign: "Have a drink on us!"[19] The fear-factions came to a screeching halt. This homeowner broke open space. At their own expense, they disrupted the polarized standoff and everyone noticed. They didn't weigh into the hostility, they didn't take sides—they simply sought connection. When I interviewed George, who is in his fifties, he said, "I'm not sure what I think about kids jumping fences, I just wanted to give those kids a drink. Now I get to say hello to them on my front lawn." Amazing! Notice that jumping the fence was not his focus, relationship was.

The world may be in a culture war, our churches may be dividing, our family members may not be talking to each other. We need a new imagination for fighting fear with love. We must refuse to enter into the terms set for us and instead seek connection. So how do we actually be with people we feel opposed to?

Reflection Questions

1. What part of Law Culture vs. Relational Culture is significant to you?

2. Do you find yourself being "judgy"? How so?

3. What step can you take to break open space in a polarized situation?

Chapter 7

MAKING MEALS FOR FRENEMIES

The stranger at the door is the living symbol . . . that we are all strangers here. . . . We were pilgrims and wanderers . . . even enemies of God, but we, too, were welcomed into this place. ◆ THOMAS G. LONG

W hat is politics? Most of the time we think of politics, we think of some mashup between a local cars salesman and a circus ringmaster. It is not a pleasant caricature we hold in our minds. The most visible picture of politics is someone running for office, airing cheesy commercial ads, placing their face on billboards off the highway, and telling us how bad the other candidate is. We use the word politics to talk about various things—institutions, conflicts, cable news, a type of discourse, and such. We even use it to speak to the internal affairs of businesses, schools, and churches when someone is "playing politics."

POWER, POWER, AND MORE POWER

Politics is ultimately about power. Who has it, how we get it, and what we do with it. I remember the politics in high school during the campaign for who would be class president. Luke Holgrum plastered fluorescent green poster boards around the school with the slogan "Vote for Me; You'll Be Happy." I don't recall life being any happier after he won the election since I still had to take the SAT, but I do remember overhearing cafeteria chatter about how cute he was, and that's why people voted for him.

What Luke was essentially saying with that clunky slogan was, "If you give me more power, I will make eleventh-grade life a little better for you." If he had lost, he apparently believed he could not make life better from his losing status. Politics (from eleventh-grade class elections all the way up to Capitol Hill) is about gaining power for the perceived good of others. It is established on the foundation that gaining power is the way to change things—even change the world. Without power, what can we do?

This has been the primary solar eclipse that has captivated American attention for centuries—candidates and political parties (usually Republicans or Democrats) fighting to gain the seat of power and eliminate the opposition's access to it. Politics is a game of power, under the notions of creating change. This culture war has forcefully shaped our understanding of how change occurs. It's like growing up in a home where your mom and dad screamed at each other all the time. You begin to think that marriage is like this. Our political imaginations are shaped by our history of politics in the US.

The phrase Religious Right refers to a loose network of political personalities and religious organizations that formed in the 1970s, also referred to as the Moral Majority associated with Jerry Falwell.[1] The Religious Right had a significant influence on the 1976, 1980, and 1988 presidential elections by directly affecting the fortunes of Jimmy Carter, Ronald Reagan, and George H. W. Bush. The formation of the Religious Right was incremental but built steam around the increasing pressure from secularists teaching Darwinian evolution in public schools, the landmark case of *Roe v. Wade*, where abortions were legalized, and the growing cultural support for same-sex marriage.

Historically, the Right has used religious language, and mostly applied it to the social issues of our day. They often referenced Genesis, the original design of man and woman (Adam and Eve) to push back gay marriage. When speaking to abortion, they used Psalm 139:13: "For you created my inmost being; you knit me together in my mother's womb." The iconic passage in Romans 1 was used often to speak to the moral decline of civilization: "For although they knew God, they neither glorified him as God nor gave thanks to him, but their thinking became futile and their foolish hearts were darkened. ... God gave them over in the sinful desires of their hearts."

The religious wing of the conservative party was passionate about gaining the power to shape policy discussions, drive voter turnout, and influence public life in the United States. They observed that America was morally eroding, and they needed to "change things." There is a logic to requiring positional power to turn back evil.

A POWERFUL RESPONSE

In reaction to this clawing, reaching, and maneuvering to gain power is growing opposition. There is a well-worn joke that has circulated the past decade that the Religious Left is rising yet it always seems to be more smoke than fire. And then 2016 happened. Granted, the core catalyst for this shift was something few expected: the election of Donald Trump. This caught many by surprise and aroused activists everywhere—a metaphorical call to arms against an enemy that threatens virtually every progressive cause. The Religious Left has their core moral issues, although very different than the Religious Right.

Jim Wallis is best known as the founder and editor of *Sojourners* magazine and has been galvanizing many young folks for political advocacy on issues of social justice since the early '90s.[2] He actively recruited voters to support President Barack Obama and eventually became a spiritual adviser to him. This action converges with the more recent organization of the Moral Movement led by the Reverend Dr. William Barber, a pastor in North Carolina. Barber has rallied a political counterpoint to the conservatives who voted Trump into office. In 2016, Governor McCrory of North Carolina lost his bid for reelection to the Democratic candidate Roy Cooper. His defeat was viewed as a victory for the Moral Movement.[3]

Their moral causes can often be described as social justice: care for impoverished groups, universal health care, equal rights for the LGBTQ community, overturning gun ownership, and affirmative action for the disadvantaged. The leading biblical imagery for their moral commitments are the accounts of Jesus advocating for the poor over the wealthy, privileged, and religious. For their moral agenda to take hold in the American landscape, they desperately need the same thing that the

Religious Right needs—to accumulate power in governing structures. In that reach for power, there has to be a winner and a loser, right?

More people than ever are asking this question: What should the role of Christians in politics be? You and I both know how Christians, right or left, begin to affiliate their political engagement with the only moral way. Political parties are built on the foundation of Us vs. Them.[4] Are we tied to this type of polarization?

The Christian outlook for change-making has been haunted and hounded by this strategy to politics for two thousand years. The disciples, all of them familiar with how politics worked, wanted to see their preferred party gain power for the moral good of the world. In their imagination, this is how change happens; the acquisition of control, or as Jesus described it, "lording over" (see Matt. 20:25 ESV).

I want to offer the disciples some slack here; they were convinced that if they obtained power, insurmountable good would be done—they would liberate Israel. This is why Peter cannot fathom Jesus being arrested.

When Jesus was in the garden of Gethsemane, a crowd of Pharisees and soldiers came carrying torches and weapons. Jesus went out and asked them, "Who is it you want?" and they replied, "Jesus of Nazareth." "Then Simon Peter, who had a sword, drew it and struck the high priest's servant, cutting off his right ear" (John 18:10). Jesus said, "Put your sword away!" (v. 11). "Am I leading a rebellion . . . ?" (Mark 14:48). For Jesus, to be taken captive is a major loss for the political revolution. Peter had a conventional understanding of political activism. To create change is to gather power and push back the enemy.

We can be just like Peter in our passions for how change-making occurs. Peter was concerned for the poor, the oppressed, and his own Jewish marginalized ethnic group. We can be just like the Pharisees who believed that morality could be legislated with more laws. We need a new imagination for change-making.

JESUS WAS KINDA POLITICAL

It's easy to paint a portrait of a Savior aloof from governmental concerns and whose teachings point to a nonpolitical life. "Christians cannot pretend they can transcend politics and simply 'preach the Gospel.'"[5] This is the typical response when we hear the words "my kingdom is not of this world" (John 18:36). We think Jesus wanted to save souls and get us out of this crummy world. In our highly charged political scene, we are often given two options for change-making. First, seek control of the national affairs through the vehicle of the Republican or Democratic Party. Second, become aloof and care less about what happens in society.

Jesus' kingdom is not of this world, but it is undoubtedly for this world.

Jesus turned down many of the avenues for gaining power: the temptations in the desert, the momentum of the crowds, even the Zealot-option. He had a different vision for change-making. It was unusual. He pioneered a peculiar way. Jesus' kingdom is not of this world, but it is undoubtedly for this world. Jesus was political, just not in the way we want Him to be.

THE POLITICS OF FOOD

Who doesn't like to eat? I do, and I think Jesus did as well. After all, He was called "a glutton and a drunkard." Meals are highlighted so frequently that theologians have noted: "Jesus ate his way through the Gospels."[6] But good eats were more than a means to fuel up. When we look a little closer at what is transpiring at the meals Jesus eats, we witness a radically different way He dwells with people. Food in the ministry of Jesus was primarily a political act.

Many of the political and religious movements of Jesus' day would not eat and dwell with each other because they differed so much. In the ancient world, eating with someone was loaded with meaning, holding powerful connotations of community. In Greek culture, an economic class system was adhered to. It was legally forbidden to mingle with those outside your economic class. Beyond the familial household, one might eat with the other members of one's district, class, or social origins.[7] Freeborn Romans, for example, did not dine with former slaves. The heads of the aristocracy invited other aristocrats to banquet with each other. Social rules of dining mirrored the sectarian structures of Greco-Roman life.[8] Table fellowship with "Them" was culturally taboo.

In first-century Judaism, there was a system of "clean and unclean." Unless the social groups consisted entirely of Jews who shared a common understanding of purity, sharing a table was out of the question. Sadducees, who were part of the aristocracy, shared meals with fellow Sadducees.[9] The Essenes were isolationists, lived in the desert, and were passionate about purity, so they would not eat with others outside their tribe. Pharisee Jews, concerned about the careful observance of Torah (and therefore exceedingly focused on regulations, before, during, and after meals), ate with other Pharisees. Zealot Jews, who advocated the forceful overthrow of the existing political order, would never sit at a table with Jews like the Sadducees, who collaborated with the occupying Roman forces.

On top of that, Jews refused to eat with Gentiles and Gentiles refused to eat with Jews—it would be an unacceptable sign of assimilation into each other's way of life.[10] In Jesus' day, the meal table is where people separated into their political tribes. It was also a site of intense scrutiny, and these political movements were closely examining Jesus for what His table fellowship revealed about His politics.

When I say "political," I mean the social structure of life. The meal table was ground zero for Jesus' new political order. Jesus' meal habits were a symbolic and practical means by which He was reframing how to live with others. Jesus was doing something supernatural at this meager piece of furniture—violating the fences between who could talk with whom. Around Jesus' table were people who would normally never sit near each other, let alone share a meal.

Jesus dwelt at numerous Pharisees' tables: Simon the Pharisee (Luke 7:36–50), an unnamed Pharisee (Luke 11:37–54), and on the Sabbath in the home of a leading Pharisee (Luke 14:1–24). He also dared to dine with Levi, a man who admits he cheated the poor to gain his wealth (Matt. 9:10–11). Jesus disrupted the gender dining etiquette as well. He supports Mary for choosing to be at the table conversation rather than confining herself to kitchen details (Luke 10:38–42).

Jesus sat at a table not as the handsome, well-groomed centerpiece of a Rembrandt painting, but as an accessible, warmhearted, spiritual troublemaker, willing to share a potluck with a household of strangers. Jesus didn't merely eat with objectionable people—outcasts and sinners—He ate with anyone, indiscriminately! The table companionship practiced by Jesus was re-creating the world, redrawing all of society's tribal maps. Jesus was disrupting the politics of His day at the table.

The early disciples were not a bunch of ignorant smelly fishermen who just fumbled from one meal to another with Jesus. They knew what was going on. They understood the table's meaning.

Jesus is taking us on a significant shift from the Old Testament into the New Testament. In Psalm 23 we encounter this well-known verse turned modern worship song: "You prepare a table before me in the presence of my enemies. You anoint my head with oil; my cup overflows." When we read that psalm, when we feel beaten down, at war with our enemy—this is a comforting text. I hear the author of this text in my own soul.

But I believe Jesus, perfect love, is inviting us beyond this heart posture. The entire ministry of Jesus deconstructs the sentiment in Psalm 23 and reconstructs an explosive idea. Jesus will prepare tables in the presence of enemies but rather than shaming them, He is inviting them. Jesus dines with tax collectors, cheaters, Pharisees, Roman soldiers, zealots, and prostitutes. This is kenotic-love in the life of Christ, making space for others unlike Him, at odds with Him, to dwell at the table. Without kenosis, we have very little tolerance or tangible room for others we fear.

HEALING AT THE TABLE

In May 2011, at about twenty thousand feet, Nadav Ben Yehuda, a twenty-four-year-old law student, was almost on top of the world. He only had three hundred more meters to go from the peak of Mount Everest, which would have made him the youngest Israeli to summit the highest mountain in the world, but something stopped him short. He noticed a man lying in the snow with no gloves, no oxygen, no shelter. Climbers know instantly twenty-six thousand feet is the "death zone" where the lack of oxygen kills even the best climbers.[11] Exposure in that zone quickly leads to acute sickness and hypothermia. Other climbers streamed past the unconscious man in the snow in their quest for the summit, but Nadav couldn't. The man was a Turkish climber named Aydin. Nadav relinquished his summit bid and sought to rescue Aydin. Nadav tied Aydin to his harness and began the descent—about a nine-hour journey to the nearest base. "It was very hard to carry him because he was heavy. At times he would gain consciousness, but then faint again. When he woke up he would scream in pain, which made it even more difficult." Because of the rescue attempt, Nadav himself suffered frostbite in four of his fingers, as well as in two toes, and lost permanent sensation in his left hand. Nadav saved the life of Aydin.

The irony of this story cannot be missed that Israel and Turkey have long been nations with relations harsher than the mountains of Everest.[12] Nadav's act not only saved a life, but also bridged a distance between two enemy countries. When asked why he relinquished his dreams of getting to the summit Nadav answered, "Because we had shared a meal together." Earlier in the trip, at base camp, at the community table, Nadav found himself sitting across from Aydin. At first it was awkward, but they began to talk and even share about their countrie's standoff with each other. This meal helped them humanize each other.

Nothing is as small but as sacred as what transpires at the table. Jesus' approach is uncomplicated. He saw people, He ate with people, and He showed them love.

VOTING OR FEASTING

The table in our mind seems to be the feeblest political act. In our culture war, we are conditioned for building a voting bloc, getting our politician into office, apprehending a majority in the Senate, and legislating change. One side believes if a progressive Democrat gets in power, our civilization will look more like the kingdom come. Another side believes if a conservative Republican gets in power, our country will be more supportive of Christian morals. The cultural assumption is that voting is the most effective means by which we make the world a better place. We believe that good and evil are at stake. It forces us to see others as political enemies to be defeated.

Sadly, in the last couple of decades, the hope for many Christians rises and falls on democracy working in their favor. I contend that voting has become an act that we've placed a disproportionate amount of hope in. We love our organizations for change—our important power centers. Yet the change-making that we desperately need, but most often neglect, will come from the up-close and unsexy space of the table.

Everything in our culture tells us to avoid this table space because it does not appear strong enough, big enough, and it does not offer us enough control.

Just fathom for a moment that God—who speaks a word and planetary systems come into existence, parts the Red Sea as if combing bed head, and makes the blind see with a simple touch of the finger—is willing to sit still at a table with messy, clumsy, irritating, and hypocritical people. Jesus stepped into the table-space with purpose; it is where God's activity is!

This is love, to embrace a posture of weakness, feeling the blunt force of human interaction, shedding all the armor, to be with people, our enemies.[13] I'm so thoroughly convinced it is in the kiln of being with those we disagree with, warts and all, at the table, that can change us. We need renewed faith that God still wants to heal the world this way, not because of our ultra-competence, but through our humble presence.

It is clear we cannot love our enemies if we skip over the plutonium power of the table.

I'm not saying you shouldn't vote, but I do want to propose that we should prioritize building tables as a better way to change the world. It is clear we cannot love our enemies if we skip over the plutonium power of the table. This is the politics of Jesus. Do you have hope that the table can change us? Are you willing to move toward your enemies at the table?

BEHOLDING OTHERS AT THE TABLE

I had decided to reach out to "frenemies" in our neighborhood who had picked up some offenses toward me, discovering them through the detached medium of Facebook. Now, it should be said that to physically be *with* our enemies is not always appropriate. If you have been physically abused or put in danger by someone, it is wise to establish a boundary until they repent. These types of choices are best discerned with trusted community. I was not in danger when I pursued my neighbors—certainly in stress, but not danger. I rattled in my skin as I invited them over for a meal. Too often we see people not as a person but as a thing. Not a potential friend but as an issue, especially if there is existing antagonism between you and the other. Who wants to eat with someone that you perceive as being fundamentally against you?

As they arrived, the meal was not ready, so I asked if they wanted to help. Suddenly we are bumping into each other, cooking together, and sharing in the mess of flour, pasta, and onion peels. I sought to expand the "Us," slowing down our urge to establish who is right and who is wrong. We must learn to be with our enemies, rather than being over them. As we sat down to eat together, things began to feel tenser. So, I asked them a question of compassionate curiosity: "How have I hurt you?"

C. S. Lewis, in his book *The Weight of Glory*, stated that next to the bread and wine, our neighbor, our enemy, is the holiest object in the world.[14] Despite how many nasty labels have been thrown around, seeing the image of God present in my polarized neighbor was the first step. Christ did more than see; He would "behold" others, and drink in with His eyes—taking in the profundity of the person before Him.[15] So much depends upon our ability to see monsters differently, as people God loves. Maybe it's conservatives, or progressives, or a neighbor, or a church member who incessantly says horrible things, who acts unjustly toward others, and plagues us whenever we see them. I know, just the sight of them causes the blood to boil.

We are each an ark, a temple of the presence of God (1 Cor. 6:19–20). Jesus is inviting us to have eyes to see. Our eyes are often looking for the presence of God in the most obvious places; in a sermon, in a worship set, in a Bible study. Or as with the prophet Elijah, in the earthquake, in the fire, but we miss Him in the gentle whisper (1 Kings 19:12). Spend less time looking for compatibility and more time beholding—looking for story, for pain, for human fragility.[16] Look past the irritants, the differences, the bothersome attributes to see the representation of God.

As this question—"How have I hurt you?"—stumbled off my tongue, I wanted to gobble it back up as if it never came out. I felt it; I was giving away the power that my ego wanted to clench tight-fisted. The more they talked, we discovered that we disagreed in some fundamental ways, but I was able to behold their pain. To freeze that moment in my mind, I see the anger and anguish in their face. This was more important to me than proving I was right in my actions. We repaired the breach between us, discovering how much more we had in common than we had in conflict. Cross the boundaries of "Us vs. Them"—try it.

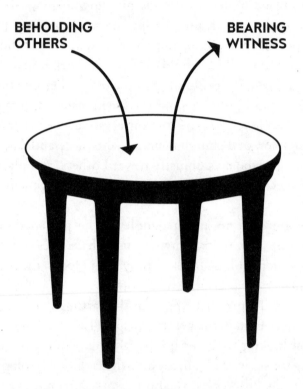

BEHOLDING OTHERS

BEARING WITNESS

BEARING WITNESS TO THE KINGDOM

Christians do not need to seek control in order to make things come out right.[17] Instead, we are invited to identify the kingdom of God in the midst of our cracked earthen encounters.

When I am beholding others at the table, I need a theology of God's active renewal. I've sat across the table from people as they've shared the atrocities as well as the complete dysfunctions of their life. It's easy to wander into hopelessness when our eyes are fixed on the horror of human brokenness. I need to know that God is near and has not abandoned us. Is God here? That question comes up for me often.

I'm drawn to moments that beguile and stir, inspire and awaken, where, for a few blissful moments, I know something special, even sacred, is happening. Where my soul gets a glimpse of what my life is all about—perhaps of what life itself is all about. It turns out this has a name: thin places. No, these are not spots to describe where skinny people hang out on the beach. Celtic Christians were deeply connected to the natural world and considered every aspect of life, especially the ordinariness of everyday life, to be infused with the presence of God.[18] They used the term "thin place" to describe this metaphysical moment in time where heaven and earth would touch, a thinner place between the sacred and the secular. Some use "thin place" to explain physical locations in the world like the wind-swept isle of Iona or the peaks of Rocky Mountains. Those are both beautiful, but perhaps God is breaking into the "thin place" between people, between enemies. We linger in a time when: wholeness and loss, healing and brokenness, liberation and injustice, life and death coexist in dynamic tension with one another. Amid dwelling with our enemies, God's kingdom is present in the paradox. If we see with polarized eyes, we can see only through the lens of good and evil. But the "thin place" is in the blur between the two, this is where we must bear witness to the kingdom.

Jesus did this often at the table, even with those who did not fully understand who He was. Long drawn out monologues or long lectures were not Jesus' style when presented with difficult subjects.[19] He did not shame; instead, He told interesting stories to illustrate the nature of the in-breaking kingdom.

USING STORY TO TELL THE TRUTH

I invited an older blue-collar mechanic over for some grilling on my back patio. We had just grilled burgers, asparagus, and were sipping on some beverages. We were basking in the humid upstate New York heat, and as typical, a fleet of police cars, sirens blaring, whizzed past our house; my new friend looked at me and said, "How do you live down here with all these hoodlums ruining the neighborhood?"

This response reminded me of when Jesus went to eat in the house of a prominent Pharisee, and a man meandered past them who was suffering from abnormal swelling of his body. Jesus took notice and decided to heal him. This disturbed the Pharisees, and they cast judgment from their perch of superiority. I sensed this was the same force at work in my new friend's judgment about my neighborhood. In response to the Pharisee's disdain, Jesus told a story of the great banquet table to illustrate the beauty of the kingdom of God. If it was good enough for Jesus, it was good enough for me. So, I told a story.

Al-amin Muhammad has eaten supper from garbage cans. Selling drugs landed him in prison. He knows what it's like to lose everything. When he got out of jail, Al-Amin had no home, no employment, and a felony that made that even more difficult. But he made a firm promise to himself: he would not sell drugs anymore. He'd spent most of his twenties and early thirties participating in gang activity in Chicago and Atlanta. Out on the streets, he struggled to find work or a place to lay his head. Drugs and alcohol became his comfort again to dull the pain. Nearly homeless for five years, he learned to find his meals in the trash, to sleep on the bus if he missed the window to get into a shelter at night.[20] More than once, he stood on a bridge and wondered if it would be better to jump.

One day, walking the streets of my city, he saw his homeless brothers and sisters and was overwhelmed by their loneliness, how they were treated like vermin. He decided he had to do something. So he posted on his Facebook page that he would be handing out sandwiches at a nearby park on a Saturday. Not sure where he was going to get the sandwiches, he was determined to offer dignity to those on the streets.

That first Saturday, a few neighbors showed up. He managed to rally a small army of people just using word of mouth. Two years later he brings together almost a hundred residents—soccer moms, scientists, social workers, elementary kids and the homeless themselves—to make sandwiches and head out together to share food. In my neighborhood, most days, the parking lot near the West Onondaga Street bridge is a place most people avoid because of the drug activity. But every Saturday, it is bursting with hope. It looks like a tailgate party.[21]

Al-amin is weaving a fabric of love and care on the streets. He wanted people to sit down and eat sandwiches together in the park, seeing faces, swapping stories, offering dignity.

I told this story, and the mood shifted. The judgment that initially hung in the air had less punch. My new friend responded, "Wow, I had no idea." Sometimes at the table, like Christ, we need to paint a picture of the better world, a world where God's kingdom is breaking in.

Sometimes at the table, like Christ, we need to paint a picture of the better world, a world where God's kingdom is breaking in.

Often at the end of Jesus' kingdom-stories we're not given any clue as to whether He changed anyone's mind.[22] I find that irritating and profound. Bearing witness to the kingdom is not about controlling outcomes but awakening imaginations. This is perhaps the exceptional brilliance of Jesus' political strategy. He doesn't grab you by the shirt and shout in your face; He doesn't pay for a commercial that slanders the opposition. He stays at the table and begins to fashion a world where we no longer see each other as foes. The table stands for a place of divine availability in the wilderness of isolating, fragmenting, polarizing American life. We are invited into the life of God, not as a museum, not as a march, but as a meal around a table with Jesus leading the conversation.

Reflection Questions

1. What part about Jesus eating and drinking with others is significant for you?

2. What part of meals being "political" brings you conflict or confusion?

3. What practical step can you take to center the table in your life?

Chapter 8

COMPASSIONATE CURIOSITY

Listening is much more than allowing another to talk while waiting for a chance to respond. Listening is paying full attention to others and welcoming them into our very beings. ◆ HENRI NOUWEN

O nce you make your mind up that you will not live in fear of your enemies, you begin to realize our culture has trained our muscles in the boxing gym of defend, debate, and destroy. We are conditioned to dig in our heels and throw a good verbal punch. If someone insults us, we insult back; if someone is snarky, we snark back; if they hate us, we hate back. We need to grow new muscles for enemy-love.

LISTENING ACROSS THE DIVIDE

I grew up in and around a version of Christianity that had very little respect for the earth. I never really heard a sermon that was anti-earth but it was just the way things were—the earth was going to burn up some day, so take that! Most of my thoughts about environmentalism were shaped in reaction to my concepts of witchcraft. My perception was that only people into witchcraft stuff cared about the earth, no, worshiped the earth. Anybody that thought we should respect it and care for it were oddballs who "worshiped and served created things rather than the Creator" (Rom. 1:25).

It wasn't until my late twenties that I began to unpack the Scriptures on this topic and pick apart its impact in my outlook on life. My journey did not start as an intellectual journey, surrounded by a library of books or even by watching Al Gore's *An Inconvenient Truth*. We didn't have much in the way of blogs and podcasts back then. I didn't even have internet access; I had to go to the library for dial up. My exploration into what God says about our relationship to the earth started with a real live person. Margaret, an Episcopal priest, befriended me.

We met up for coffee almost every Tuesday morning. Her office always carried the smell of vanilla candle, and the soothing sounds of her favorite instrumental music playing from her early '90s edition boom box. Every time I sauntered into her office, she asked if would like coffee and a "tasty treat," which was dipping my hand into a bulk-size bucket of animal crackers she bought at Costco. We had a peculiar relationship: a sixty-something ordained woman and a twenty-seven-year-old youth pastor. Our worlds were different in so many ways. We talked about all sorts of things, but mostly she asked me questions.

I had never had anyone ask me the sorts of questions she asked. And it wasn't just the questions; it was the way she asked them. She asked questions like "Dan, how does it feel when someone only sees you as a pastor and not a person?" I never had clear answers because I had never been in touch with those thoughts and feelings before. Always, always, as I was trying to find precise words for her careful questions, she was leaning forward, in genuine suspense, eyes that didn't seem to blink, curious about my answers. At times her blue eyes looked so intently that it felt like a laser pointer was hovering on my face.

We barely talked about "environmentalism." In the back of my mind she was an earth-hippie. She was always sensitive to the use of plastic and even bought me a reusable water bottle so that I wouldn't buy and throw away plastic ones. She asked me if I had ever considered riding my bike to work since I lived so close. "You know, you'll save a little pollution if you do." I didn't really understand her for the longest time.

But one day she asked me if it was okay if she could read something out loud to me. I said sure. "In the beginning God created the heavens and the earth. . . . God said, 'Let there be light,' and there was light. . . . God called the light 'day,' and the darkness he called 'night.' . . . God made the vault and separated the water under the vault from the water above it. And it was so. . . . 'Let the land produce vegetation: seed-bearing plants and trees on the land that bear fruit.' . . ." She read the whole first chapter of Genesis. Near the end of her reading I noticed that she was crying a bit. I asked "Margaret, are you okay?" She looked up and said "Can you imagine putting so much love and labor into something so beautiful and then people treat it like rubbish? This planet is not trash to God, it's a treasure." I was speechless.

I remember driving back to my office after our meet-up that day and at one point saying to myself, "Have I missed something?" We were a bit polarized theologically, but her inquisitive and affectionate posture began to soften my thoughtless positions about the earth. I pondered, *How could God start the story of the world with such care and tenderness and then end it with such carelessness and destruction?* Something seemed off. This began my study.

I discovered the great arc of Scripture. From Genesis to Revelation, the Creator of the world is bringing new creation. God is not going to abolish the universe of space, time, and matter; He is going to renew it, to restore it, to fill it with new joy and delight. God's original intentions in Genesis 1 are not scrapped because of the fall in Genesis 3. Instead God goes to great lengths to recover everything derailed by sin and selfishness. God is renewing all things. I'd like to give you proof texts to support this narrative but that will not do it justice. The whole counsel of Scripture is arcing toward renewal. Renewal of our relationship with God, with each other, *and* with the earth. How come I never saw any of this before?

Whether you agree with my biblical shift or not isn't my direct point. I became open to something that I previously feared because of Margaret's affectionate presence. Specifically, her compassion and curiosity were the ladder over our polarized fence. Our fears of each other naturally shape us for un-listening. We perceive that we have the "monsters" all sized-up; we label them and categorize them. This is why the ministry approach of Jesus is so world-altering. I did ask Margaret, years later, if she just wanted to tell me straight out "you're damaging the earth and you're wrong, you little whippersnapper!" Her response: "I figured you'd already heard that argument. I'd rather spend my time building a friendship and softening the hard ground between us." I felt the hard ground, she watered it, and it did become a little softer.

GOD ASKING QUESTIONS

Jesus, all-knowing God, Creator of the cosmos, who's numbered every hair on our heads—asks questions, lots of them. More questions proceed from Jesus' mouth than answers. Jesus asks 307 questions to be exact.[1] Asking questions was central to Jesus' work of befriending. It is a kind of listening that is not defensive, not critical, not suspicious. It is the opposite of the kind of listening that a jury does when listening to a witness on the stand, or the kind of listening a spouse does to catch their partner in a communication error. It should unsettle us that a God who knows everything uses questions as His main mode of being with others.

Whether in a public gathering, in the presence of His enemies, or a private conversation with His closest friends, Jesus consistently used questions to open new possibilities. Jesus was not just looking for the swapping of information; He was seeking connection. In Luke 9:18 we get a classic example of Jesus using a question to unearth something deeper, "Who do the crowds say I am?" Why did Jesus ask this? Did He not know?[2] Jesus embraced some limits. My hunch though is that Jesus was genuinely curious—He desired to discover those around Him and help them discover what was deep within them.

Peter responds to that initial question with one of the most profound statements in the entire Bible: "You are the Christ, the Son of the living God" (Matt. 16:16 NKJV). Curiosity helps coax the heart out of hiding. The heart likes to stay cloaked, the realities we accept like to linger in the shadows, and the lies that we keep like to remain unnamed. We can easily be fooled by the physical or political presentations of another. Jesus moves past appearances. Jesus is more interested in ushering the soul into the daylight. Why is it not a habit to be curious about each other? Could it be we think we have each other figured out? Could it be that we want control of what's being said?

SEEKING CONTROL

Our society doesn't like questions because we are into control—questions are not safe. Watch cable news for a few minutes, and you see pundits shouting down each other, talking over one another, arguing point for point. Our polarized culture has heat-seeking missiles for gaining control in a conversation. It is seen as a sign of strength. The mic drop symbolizes our polarizing times.

Jesus seems to lack an agenda of gaining control in every conversation He finds Himself in. He's genuinely okay asking "Who do people say I am?" and waiting for the answer. Ask a question, and you have no idea what kind of answer you might get. Jesus doesn't need to prove He is right to be right. Curiosity gives away power to another. It is an acknowledgment that we don't know everything. This assumes humility, that we don't already know the motivations that lurk behind other beliefs, statements, or positions within the heart.

Curiosity pushes us to more, answers tell us we're done. Think about it . . . once you have the answer, you're finished. Answers are satisfying and provide us psychological return.[3] If you're someone that tends to have a lot of answers, you may see the work of curiosity as a waste of time—you've already appraised the person in front of you. Curiosity is the art of learning that places us at the feet of another for a moment, humbly, seeking a more in-depth story past perceived stereotypes. We cannot discover someone's story if we have already decided someone's narrative.[4] We are wandering into the unexplored, we are not Napoléon Bonaparte conquering others; rather, we are seeking to discover others.

As an introvert, I have been on a journey myself in cultivating curiosity toward others. I'd fully enjoy living in a cabin in Madagascar, off the grid, without any technology. Staying to myself is my happy place. When we bought our first home seventeen years ago I didn't know what to do with myself when I was mowing the lawn and my neighbor was out in his yard at the same time. Do I just wave? Am I obligated to go over and talk to him? Is it possible to pretend that he's not there?

When we first connected, it was obvious we had very little in common. He was raised in the sticks, twenty-five years older than me, and into bass fishing. Sitting in a boat at 6 a.m., stabbing worms with a hook, in hopes that we might catch something, anything—misery.

Something began to transpire between us as we connected. Walter had a story. He shared his love for fishing, and how it connected him to his dad who had passed away. He shared his Catholic upbringing, how it made him appreciate prayer. He shared about his grown son, how he was afraid he wasn't a good dad. There were moments when Walter would say things like "I've never told anybody this" or "I can't believe I just told you that." I learned to ask questions, better questions, curious questions, like: "Walter, when you mow the lawn, what do you think about?" or "Walter, how does fishing make you feel?" Sometimes his responses made me cringe, and other times they took my breath away. Curiosity introduced me to the treasure of Walter. He was a gift that started me on the path of discovering others.

CURIOSITY IS DANGEROUS

In some ways we believe we're curious because we scour for information daily by asking questions like, "Hey Google, how much sugar is in a liter of Mountain Dew?" We ask more questions to robots than we do the humans around us. But genuine curiosity toward those who believe differently than us, live differently than us, worship differently than us—it's a scarce attribute. Curiosity is always dangerous.

Within history, there have been world leaders and forces that have sought to snuff out curiosity: Fidel Castro, Mao Zedong, Joseph Stalin. The Taliban destroyed works of art. ISIS burns works of literature in villages in the Middle East.[5] The Nazis degenerated art exhibits where they tried to deface all modern paintings. During the Middle Ages, curiosity was almost taken out of existence because the established church wanted to convey to the masses that everything worth knowing is already known. Being curious is a powerful disrupter in the face of fear.

Being curious about information is essential, but being curious about each other is an act of defiance! The powers and principalities of polarization tell us how to think daily: "they are anti-American," "they are anti-woman," "they are rapists," "they are ignorant," "they are thugs." Our culture force-feeds us these labels, categorizes people, so we no longer need to be curious about each other. We inhabit a war zone of rhetoric.

TALK, TALK, TALK

You probably talk too much—we all do. Talking isn't the big problem, it's what science has exposed as our favorite subject— ourselves. One researcher reports that "on average, people spend

60 percent of conversations talking about themselves—and this figure jumps to 80 percent when communicating via social media platforms such as Twitter or Facebook."[6] Researchers found that there is a dopamine effect, it just feels better. Talking about ourselves gives us a neurological buzz. We often tend to focus more on impressing others with our persona, our education, our eloquence, or our stories. We become absorbed with "I did this . . . I did that . . . I like this . . . I've been there" and offering bits of information to see if anyone will find them fascinating. It takes mindfulness to shake off the anxious need to be recognized and celebrated by the other. Believing Jesus already sees you, loves you, and affirms you, frees you up to see others—to be interested in them. I've learned that being interested is much more enjoyable than my own attempts to appear interesting.

I've learned that being interested is much more enjoyable than my own attempts to appear interesting.

ASK QUESTIONS, SIT SILENT

I was a chaplain for a few years and consistently found myself in the midst of people's pain, in hospital rooms, by their bedside, or sitting on the steps outside their house. There was a voice within my head that told me, "Say something brilliant." Not sure where it came from, but it felt like I needed to fix with my advice or eliminate the awkwardness with my words. Gradually I learned that being silent, alongside, in moments of vulnerable suffering, needs no elegant language.

Silence gives us space for a relational exchange that leads to healing. In a world where everyone wants to be heard, one of the greatest acts of love we can offer is to be silent, make eye contact, and listen. Can we embrace this posture in the face of those we deem our enemies, the "them"?

WE ALL SUFFER

The actual word "curiosity" derives from Latin word *cūriōsitās*, which means "careful." To be curious is to believe that everyone, yes everyone, should be treated with carefulness. Curiosity is a disruptive practice, but when combined with compassion it is downright divine. Compassion consists of two parts: "co," which means *together*, and "passion," which means *suffering*. When we believe in "co" we believe both of us, all of us, even my enemy, is in the same predicament.

I'm going to let you in on a little secret: you're suffering. Are you not? If you say no, you're either not from this planet or transcended being human. To be human is to suffer. Whether big or small, everyone is struggling with something, no matter how masked it may be, no matter how many façades we hide behind. We're all hurting, some of us just pretend we're not.

A few years back I began having problems sleeping. The problem progressed, and I fell into a rut of insomnia. I tried every trick in the book, a glass of wine before bed, hot baths, massages, special lighting—nothing worked. Going to bed triggered anxiety, and I would panic at the anguish the night inevitably would bring. Every night at 2:00 a.m. I'd find myself crying and cussing as I lay on various surfaces: the couch, the kitchen floor, the porch, even my car one desperate night. I went to sleep clinics, saw kinesiologists, and even had someone attempt to cast a demon out of me. I was powerless, but I kept up my appearances. No one but my wife knew how desperate and dark my life was becoming. I masked my suffering in niceties when people asked, "How are you doing, Dan?"

When I finally found myself in the hospital, I couldn't hide it any longer. The consistent response from friends who visited me was "I had no idea."

That circumstance in my life revealed something to me—people hide their suffering. Indeed my pain is not as severe as the genocide occurring in Sudan or the brutality on women in Yemen. Though in the midst of my suffering, if you had told me, "other people have it worse," I'd have been tempted to flip you the bird. Our suffering, no matter what it is, feels unbearable. Our pain is what we have in common. We need curiosity to discover it in each other.

When we look at our enemies, those who we're polarized against, we can begin to believe we are nothing like them—seeing them more as a monster than as a fellow human. This "co" part of compassion means we are all struggling with the human experience. We're all colliding painfully with our powerlessness to apprehend happiness—this being human thing is not easy.

Many of the things that bother you, even anger you, about other people are their attempts to deal with difficult existential situations. We desire happiness, and don't experience it. We desire to be free from pain, and yet feel trapped in it. Their moods, their clinging, their outbursts, their hatreds—all of these are the results of human beings grasping for control over their lives.

COMPASSION HAS NO ENEMIES

At one point, a high-ranking centurion sent a messenger to approach Jesus and asked for healing on behalf of his servant (Luke 7:1–10). During the New Testament era, a Roman centurion was a professional military officer commanding a platoon of troops called a "century." Jewish people feared them as they were the most visible presence of Roman oppression. They were often stationed throughout towns to keep order, symbolizing the watching eye of Caesar.

This centurion has the authority to command Jesus to come, but he doesn't leverage it. He merely shares that his servant is sick, at the point of death, and loved by him greatly. Jesus recognizes his pain, his suffering, although he is the "Them" in the eyes of the oppressed Jews. Jesus goes to heal him. For God, compassion has no borders, no fences, no Us vs. Them.

Pain is a universal language. Recognizing this invites us to see beyond difference, beyond appearances, beyond politics to the essence, the *tselem*, the image of God. Those I fear, that seem like monsters, are bombarded by pain, different pain, but nevertheless, pain. When we find ourselves constricting our compassion, we are not following in the way of Jesus. Jesus offers compassion to the human person, unbounded love to everyone, even His enemies.

THE COMPASSIONATE CURIOSITY PATH

At one point in my life, I had a daily forty-five-minute drive to work on a four-lane highway. The traffic was horrible and could stir up a hearty portion of irritation. The noise, the horns blaring, the constant braking, that one driver using that three-foot buffer between your car and another to thread a needle. By the time I got to work, I had needed to make sure I didn't talk to someone immediately because they would be the target of my pent-up rage.

The highway passed through a small patch of a densely wooded area and off the side of the road I could see a dirt footpath. Most days I noticed it out of the corner of my eye and thought, *Wonder where that goes?* One day on my way to work, seeing it for the hundredth time, I decided to pull off onto the shoulder and explore it—cars whizzing past, eighteen-wheelers honking at me. I tepidly began to walk down that dirt path mostly overgrown with brush. Suddenly I noticed how quiet and still everything was and the private pond appeared. This beautiful, serene pond, the sun reflecting off it, an older gentleman fishing, and the ducks enjoying a swim. In the midst of the concrete jungle, this beautiful treasure exists.

This is my experience with the work of Compassionate Curiosity. It is like taking this unnoticed path in the midst of the noise and bombast. We must stop, take interest, and make the journey down the path. What follows is the tangible compassionate curiosity path I've been practicing for a while now. It's certainly not perfect, but it has opened my life up to healing conversations in our polarized times.

BE INTERESTED

Birds of the same feather flock together. We typically are interested in others who have something to offer us or have something in common with us. To be interested we need to notice the dirt path off the side of the four-lane highway of our lives. We need to look for peculiar things in people, things unlike us that draw our curiosity.

Jesus went out of His way to show interest in people across the divide. The most obvious occasion was His conversation with the woman at the well. He took His disciples on a journey through Samaria when typically, a rabbi and his Jewish followers would take a long way around. Jesus desired to connect with Samaritans. This must have seemed bizarre to His followers when they sat down at Jacob's well outside of Sychar.

We are magnets for "likeness" but Jesus was a magnet for

"differents." God invites us to go where we ordinarily would not desire to go. To show interest in people we usually feel polarized against.

One of my neighbors is a fun fellow who isn't afraid to share whatever urgent thought comes into his head. When I'm walking my dog, I always make it a point to stop at his house and say hello. He recently said, "If we legalized marijuana, we'd have fewer arrests." This interested me. It's not something I'd typically subscribe to. So, I said, "Tell me a bit more about that." His reply was, "Why is a pastor interested in marijuana? Is the parish life hard on ya, Pastor?" Often when I find something different, rather than reacting in contempt or disgust, I move toward them with curiosity. Our points of difference can either be barriers or bridges. There is always something genuinely interesting about someone unlike you. Everyone has a story to be discovered.

BE INQUISITIVE

When we pause our reactions of attacking or avoiding, what's next? Learn to ask questions. Questions might seem like a passive instrument, but in a hostile world, they are more like a pry-bar that opens the soul. When you find yourself about to make a statement, turn it into a question.[7] For example, before stating, "This steak is really good" instead ask, "What makes this steak really good?" Then listen for answers or look for answers yourself. You'll start to notice things you never did before. Do that with your encounters.

Sitting next to a stranger, sipping on a drink at our local watering hole, I glanced at the fellow sitting next to me enjoying his juicy burger. He said, "This is a great bar." I asked him why he thought it was a great bar. He seemed a bit caught off

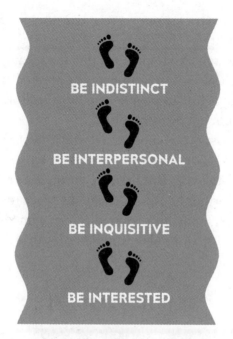

COMPASSIONATE CURIOSITY PATH

guard by the question. Awkwardly he responded with, "Well I'm from out of town, and it's hard to find a good place to watch the game sometimes." Typically banter in a bar is kept strictly to sports and shouting TVs. I asked him what brought him to our city. "I'm here for therapy," he sheepishly respond-ed. "Therapy has been beneficial in my life; how has it been helpful in yours?" He turned to me directly, slightly offended, and said, "Really dude, you want to know about my past? I doubt it!" At this point, I felt the stiff arm. So I took one more attempt and said, "Sure, I'm all ears." In the midst of blasting TVs and craft beer, he let slip out, "I'm getting therapy because I'm a registered sexual offender." Over the next two hours, we found ourselves sharing our regrets, our need for change, and our shame about our choices in life. We missed the entire game we came to watch. A momentous divine exchange occurred. At one point he said, "To most people I'm repulsive." I imagine Jesus sitting close to people who by all cultural standards are repulsive but not being repulsed.

Asking questions is more transformative than giving answers. That does not mean that answers are irrelevant. We find answers along the way. But first, we must create a pathway to walk upon. Curious questions create the space for something new to emerge, something unpredictable, something new to arise between us; all kinds of possibilities that did not exist before.

BE INTERPERSONAL

Too often we are preoccupied with our to-do list, checking our phones, and mulling over better ways to spend our time. Sure, we are physically present, but our attention span is in another universe.[8] With regularity someone asks me a question, I begin to squeak out some words, and they are already glancing at their phone or disinterested, looking around the room.

To be interpersonal we need to take our five senses—taste, sight, touch, smell, and sound—captive in the moment of conversation. Jesus uses all five senses to be present with others. He uses the sense of taste, purposely feasting with others, picking up the reputation of being a glutton. Using food for more than nourishment but connection. He uses the sense of sight, looking intently for a woman that touches the edge of His robe. He does not accept the cursory answer the disciples give Him: "You're in a crowd, what do You expect?" (see Luke 8:45). Jesus used the sense of touch when people brought Jesus a deaf man.

Jesus healed the man, of course, but interestingly, by putting His fingers in the man's ears and touching the man's tongue. Jesus also uses smell; coming upon the gravesite of His friend Lazarus, Martha says, "Lord, he has been dead for four days. The smell will be terrible" (John 11:39 NLT). He enters into the stench of suffering and loss. Finally, Jesus uses the sense of sound, listening to the cries of the demon-possessed man cutting himself with stones. The disciples probably wanted to run, but Jesus asks the man, "What is your name?" (Mark 5:9).

To be interpersonal we bring all our senses to a singular place at a precise moment. Our bodies struggle with undivided attention. As one who has diagnosed ADHD, holding my attention in one place does not come naturally. What has been remarkable is that over time, because of the goal of compassionate curiosity, I have been able to retrain my senses incrementally: expressing warmth in a firm hug, making eye contact, sitting still, asking careful questions, listening intently, and verbalizing what I am hearing.

BE INDISTINCT

It is fascinating that Jesus doesn't preach three-point sermons that lay out His airtight case for why He is right. He hardly puts the philosophical smack down on His doubters. Many of Jesus' detractors are looking for a verbal sparring match, coming at Him with accusations and arguments. Instead of retorts and well-defended statements, He meets their assaults with more and more questions and stories. How frustrating? Right!

In Mark 4:10–11 it says, "When he was alone, the Twelve and the others around him asked him about the parables. He told them, 'The secret of the kingdom of God has been given to you. But to those on the outside everything is said in parables.'" I'd probably have been with the disciples on this one. "Jesus, why are You doing this? You're telling stories but nobody is getting Your point." The disciples are frustrated by His subjective parable-telling methods.[9] Why not just make it plain-speak? It has always puzzled me. Why does Jesus seemingly indicate He doesn't want to be clear?

I have a working theory on this. Parables (stories) serve as a kind of curiosity-creating technique. Parables tuck the treasure beneath the surface, out of the reach of those who seek knowledge, not transformation. Some people will listen, and it sparks questions. If Jesus told it straight, there is no exploration required. He is enticing listeners to tune their ears to a different frequency.

I suspect if the disciples had not asked Jesus about the parables, He may not have explained them. The subterraneous meaning of the kingdom of God is found through the gateway of being inquisitive. Could this be where it starts? Those who ask Jesus for further explanation are the ones to whom the deeper meaning is revealed.

If Jesus were walking the earth today, He might be called elusive, ambiguous, and hard to pin down. He'd probably be unwilling to provide concise sound bites for public consumption on CNN or *Good Morning America*. Matthew's gospel records the peculiar way in which Jesus speaks to injustice and unrighteousness: "He will not quarrel or cry out; no one will hear his voice in the streets" (12:19). These words point to the pervading calmness of the way of Jesus, which stood out in marked contrast to the wrangling of Jewish scribes, the violence of Roman officers, and the proclaiming prophets in the streets.

As you are conversing with those you might be polarized with, resist the urge to be clear and combative. Yeah, you heard me right. Is it ever okay to be ambiguous? I believe it is, because Jesus was, quite often. Is it ever okay to come across unclear? I believe it is, because Jesus sometimes was. Is it ever okay to not give a Yes or No to the "is it a sin" question? Yes, because often the history of that question is so convoluted with agendas. As the philosopher Slavoj Zizek says, "We cannot understand each other's Yes or No answers because there is a world of antagonism sitting atop them."[10]

This reminds of a weird or interesting conversation (depends on your interpretation) I had with someone recently at our local coffee shop. While sitting at the bar, making small talk, a woman asked me "Do you think Kevin Spacey is a good actor?" "Sure, he was really good in the movie *Pay It Forward*." Quickly she retorted, "So you're for sexual assault!" I backpedaled and shared that I wasn't, but I did think he was a good actor. The conversation halted. Listening and presence eroded like a sandcastle in a tsunami. The conversation was over. The reality is that our yes or no answers are wound tight in antagonism. If we care to be present, to converse, to be together long enough to trust one another, we will take that into deep consideration.

Being indistinct is not a dodge nor is it a slippery slope. To be indistinct we are extending space for us to see each other, explore each other, and understand each other.[11] The work of connection takes priority rather than efficiency of clarity. Does this mean we don't hold convictions? I do. You do. Of course we do. Convictions are not the problem; our postures with each other are. In order to build the bridge of listening to each other, relearn how to stay still and stay curious. To be indistinct is to be at peace not being heard, seen, or acknowledged for the opinions I hold. This is an act of humility. There is a time for clarifying your points and positions, but it is a mistake to do this before building a relational bridge through compassionate curiosity.

In hotly divided times, where fear is the primary emotion between us, the act of listening is the first thing to get pitched in the dumpster. It may seem like a weak weapon in the face of monsters, but don't underestimate the power of compassionate curiosity to dismantle the antagonism between us.

Reflection Questions

1. We all suffer. How does this change our postures toward each other?

2. What part of "asking questions" is difficult for you?

3. What practical step can you take to move along the Curiosity Path?

Chapter 9

THE AIKIDO OF FORGIVENESS

Hatred tends to dry up the springs of creative thought in the life of the hater, so that his resourcefulness becomes completely focused on the negative aspects of his environment. ◆ HOWARD THURMAN

The power in the martial art of aikido comes from a strategic noncombative posture. If you have ever watched martial arts footage and seen a person abscond, tuck, and reemerge, calm and smiling and in a stronger position before the attacker even realizes they're gone, you have been viewing the art of aikido.[1] Aikido is a way to fight, with no kicks, no punches. It deals with how to absorb a kick, how to take a punch, redirect energy, go down, and rise up stronger.

It is the hardest of all the martial arts to learn, in part because it is teaching the body and the mind what thousands of years of conditioning has trained us not to do—to relax when we feel threatened, to maintain control of our internal energies. In the face of an attack, our primal instinct is to tighten up.[2] There is a part of us that attacks and reacts faster than the part of our brain that can slow down and contemplate action.

Wendy Palmer, one of the most prominent aikidoists, is only 5'5" and 135 pounds but is able to neutralize men twice her size. There is a counterintuitive nature to it all. "We think we need to exercise our power by meeting the blunt force of power with aggressive power," says Palmer.[3] We claim our power by training our bodies and neurological pathways to an alternative approach to fighting.

Forgiveness is not natural, nor understood intuitively as the claiming of power. Aikido embodies this idea that when we stop meeting something with like-force, we can stop giving it power. We neutralize it, we disrupt it. In aikido, an uke (the person who receives an attack) absorbs and transforms the incoming aggressive energy.[4] If boxing is about meeting force with force, then aikido is about redirecting force. The goal in boxing is to be stronger and more violent than your attacker, bloodying up yourself in the process of offering blow after blow. The goal in aikido is to frustrate the violence of your attacker, eventually exhausting them, and neutralizing them.[5] Forgiveness is not giving yourself over to the attacker; it's giving yourself over to another way of being. A way that disempowers the threat.

UPSIDE-DOWN TACTICS

What does the aikido of forgiveness look like in the face of fear? Is it just a mental state? Jesus unfolds three examples that were much more than sentimental or mental. Jesus prescribes a way of love that can physically and emotionally disrupt the polarization we find ourselves in. He unleashes three wild solutions in the Sermon on the Mount (Matt. 5:39–41):

1. "If anyone slaps you on the right cheek, turn to them the other cheek . . ."

2. "If anyone wants to sue you and take your shirt, hand over your coat as well . . ."

3. "If anyone forces you to go one mile, go with them two miles."

All three initial aggressive actions would naturally provoke an aggressive *reaction*, something like: "If someone slaps you on the cheek, slap them right back," or "If someone sues you for your cloak, spit on it then throw it back," or "If a jerk tells you to carry their pack, tear them apart verbally the whole time." Not enough can be said about how these proposed solutions by Jesus would sound like an absurdity to those being kicked around by the Roman Empire. They sound asinine to us in the real world of playground bullies or abusive bosses or oppressive regimes or violent extremists. Jesus, who lived in a society that barely had any memory of peace, was offering an *upside-down* tactic to facing unfair treatment.[6] This enemy-love teaching is unique for its time, and it has been ever since. Jesus is addressing our instinct to treat enemies like enemies, which only creates enemy-like reactions.

Jesus is addressing our instinct to treat enemies like enemies, which only creates enemy-like reactions.

The most popular usage of these three tactics in the Sermon on the Mount has done a great disservice to their disruptive power. Typically, "walking the extra mile" is code for staying to clean up the mess after the party. And "turning the other cheek" is code for biting your tongue when someone says means things to you. This entire section of Jesus' words has become domesticated for easy swallowing.

TURN THE OTHER CHEEK

What is going on here? Jesus specifically clarifies the "right cheek." The left hand in the first-century world was used only for unclean bathroom tasks (if you know what I mean). There were two ways to hit somebody: a punch with a right fist or a backhanded slap with the right hand. A slap is how you hit someone who was beneath you—a master to a slave, and a Roman soldier to a Jewish citizen.[7] Jesus says, "If anyone slaps you on the right cheek, turn to them the other cheek also." Do you realize what's going on here?

To be slapped or backhanded is to be treated subhuman. But in "turning the other cheek" you are requiring your enemy to punch you. A punch was for equals. So if they want to hit you again, they would have to look you in the eye and hit you as an equal.[8] You are triggering something that the enemy is not anticipating, and you force the enemy to see you differently . . . a human being with dignity. Jesus exceeds combating our enemy into awakening our enemy.

TAKE OFF YOUR CLOTHES

And Jesus keeps the aikido solutions coming! "And if anyone wants to sue you and take your shirt, hand over your coat as well" (Matt. 5:40). When someone sued you for your shirt, they were taking everything you had because you couldn't pay your debts. A coat or "cloak" (KJV) was the outer garment, like a blanket, that was worn to keep warm. If someone sued you for your shirt, you'd be left standing in your coat. Jesus then says, "Hand over your coat as well." Now you get the picture—you're standing there in your birthday suit for all to see. Suddenly your enemy is standing over your naked body, confronted with his own violent actions.[9]

WALK THE EXTRA MILE

The last doozy—Jesus says go the extra mile. The audience Jesus is speaking to has a boot on their neck, upwards to 80% of their income is taken from them in taxes, which keeps them in poverty.[10] According to Roman law, a soldier could command you to carry their gun and gear, so you had to submit. The law limited it to one mile as to prevent soldiers from creating permanent servants on the road.[11] Imagine you could be out getting kosher pizza with the family, and a soldier says, "Hey, get over here, carry my stuff." This humiliation of being treated like an animal, in front of your whole family. Jesus says when this happens to you, keep going after the one-mile mark. The moment you enter into the second mile. What is going on? Who holds the power now?

FROM REACTIVE TO ACTIVE

We have dehumanized each other in our polarizing times, and forgiveness can confront us with seeing the humanity of each other—creating a new type of relationship between enemies. Forgiveness is not passive or laissez-faire; it is fiercely engaged: "I am willing to forgive, but I want you to see me as valuable, as divinely human." All three of these radical options given by Jesus are disruptive. They are statements that "I will not devolve into your way of speaking, of hurting, of mocking, of gossiping, of shaming, or humiliating," nor "will I repay evil with evil but evil with good." This is a refusal to keep the polarization in circulation.

Jesus is illustrating that forgiveness is not reactive, but it is active. There is a difference between reaction and action, meaning that action is having a thoughtful, self-controlled, presence in a situation while reaction follows the polarized agenda set by somebody else, falling into their trap. We are being socialized for *reaction* by cable news, Facebook, and Twitter—maybe even by our nuclear families. This reactive posture is certainly cathartic, like a pressure relief valve, but it is not by any means transforming anyone.

TELLING A NEW STORY

Jesus is inviting His disciples into writing a new story, a new way of engagement, powered by forgiveness. We cannot choose what hurt and pain happen to us, but we can always choose how to relate to what happens to us.[12] Part of forgiveness is finding a new story to live by rather than the one given to us by those who hurt us, gossip about us, oppose us, lie about us, and hate us. Living by the old story draws us into the same practices that hurt us.

Leaving the standoff of "Us vs. Them" means shifting from the status of the victim to the one voluntarily pouring out love. This shift is a shift of power. Power does not emanate from someone with the loudest mouth or the biggest sword; it originates from the agency of love ignited by God's Spirit.

To live in a new story, we must see ourselves differently.[13]

In all three illustrations of the aikido of forgiveness, the power dynamic is visible: oppressed and oppressor, or accused and accuser, or victim and victimizer, or offended and offender. But Jesus is reframing the story, the characters, and their roles. Typically, the one who has been wronged rehearses their offenses, over and over and over again. This replay is our grievance story that stirs up our Crock-Pot of desire for vindication.

Psychologist Joan O'C Hamilton explains this story:

> Initially, a grievance story is simply one's version of what happened. But over time, it can become something more malignant—a detail-packed, often obsessively repeated, subtly or not-so-subtly distorted account that embellishes the role of a villain who is responsible for one's misery.[14]

Researcher Fred Luskin states, "The problem with our stories is they always focus on 'them'—the other person—and why he won't change or what she won't do. That gives them power they shouldn't have."[15] The constant focus and attention on the insult and the offender gives them absolute power over us; they rule the story. Who rules your story? Do you want to live by the narrative of vindication and vengeance rather than generosity and grace? I concede there is a moral high when we punish someone who has wronged us. But it is an addiction like crack cocaine that will string us along into death.

Jesus is flipping the story of who holds power. Forgiveness is not powerlessness; it actually might be the only thing powerful enough to transform your enemy.[16] Jesus is giving us insight into the monsters. We see them as desperate, as one who stands before you and pleads, without actually saying it,

"Help me, give me the one thing that can overcome my hate, my fear, give me love, the love of Jesus."[17] When we become the forgiver, we begin to disrupt the cycle of who holds power.

RELEASING GOODNESS

To forgive could feel like surrender, a retreat in the context of a battle. But Jesus offers us forgiveness not as a white flag but as a weapon. Wonder of wonders—God suffered for us instead of exacting suffering upon His enemies. Jesus absorbed our sin, our grief, and our injuries. We begin to see ourselves dealing with others the way God deals with us, releasing goodness—full of compassion, flowing in mercy. It is not God's judgment but God's kindness that leads to repentance, a change of heart (Rom. 2:4).

Jesus offers us forgiveness not as a white flag but as a weapon.

Can forgiveness change our enemies?

Shauna Hodges has experimented with the aikido of forgiveness first hand. She woke one morning, peered out the window, and was startled by the oversized Confederate flag waving on her neighbor's porch. Shauna and her neighbor Mike had always been on different pages politically, creating some awkwardness in their exchanges, but never in conflict. Shauna is a black churchgoing mother. Mike is an Irish churchgoing grandfather. Shauna is single, and her house is filled with baby toys, piled-up dishes in the sink, and Cheerios littering the floor from her two-year-old.

Mike's home is filled with memories from his life—pictures of his grandkids, a medal of honor hanging over the fireplace mantel, and his well-worn recliner where he reads the Sunday newspaper. They come from different worlds and conveniently stayed out of each other's way, but this flag hanging on Mike's porch really stung Shauna; a daily reminder of slavery every time she walked outside. She did not want her child to see it on a regular basis. What could she do?

She asked her church small group for counsel. Enraged, a few of them began to plan how to rip it down under cover of night. A few others said to "just ignore it," and maybe he'll take it down after a while. None of their answers resonated.

With courage and kindness, she walked across the street to have a conversation. He did not answer the doorbell; with trembling hands she scribbled a note and left it: "Hi neighbor, I'd like to invite you over to get a cup of coffee, and chat about your flag." She carried a pit in her stomach as she waited for his response; two long weeks went by.

As she was taking a walk with Gracian, her son, on a Saturday afternoon, she noticed him pull into his driveway, so she bolted to his house like the paparazzi. She was there with a forced smile to greet him as he exited his car. Mike made it clear he was not interested in connecting. She pressed, "I'm not your enemy; I just want to talk." He relented, "Fine, tomorrow."

Knocking on his door the next day, she wished she had never started pushing this snowball down the hill; it felt bigger than she was. As he let her in, she saw the signs of life, pictures of grandchildren, newspapers stacked, and war paraphernalia on the walls.

They talked for an hour, nibbled on muffins she baked, laughed some, and shared about kids, and grandkids and eventually talked about the flag. He was stubborn, but she was able to unfold a bit of why it hurt her. Relenting halfway, "I'll take it down for you, even though it doesn't make a lick of sense." A few days later, the flag came down. Shauna put a little gift basket on his porch, with a blueberry pie, and another note: "I want you to know how much it means to me." Over that following year, a relationship began to sprout. He shoveled her driveway once when she was snowed in. He even offered to watch her kid if she ever needed a break.

In an urgent moment, she took him up on his offer, while Gracian was taking a nap. When she came home to relieve Mike of his babysitting duties, Gracian was still sleeping, they lingered awkwardly at the dining room table. Mike broke the ice: "I've been thinking about the flag thing." He began to see that the flag communicated racism. Then the bombshell: "Honestly Shauna, you are the first black person I've been friends with." Mike was reconsidering who he was and who she was. Shauna's overtures of affection had started breaking the cycle of polarization.

From the outset, Shauna had decided she would forgive him for his disparaging feelings toward black folks, the unknowing insensitive remarks that leaked out of his mouth. Christ's words rang in her ears: "Father, forgive them, for they do not know what they are doing." Though she initially feared him, she sought to disrupt him with friendship. She positively spoke truth to him, but it was wrapped in connection and compassion. This changed his world.

RIGHTEOUS TABLE-FLIPPING

Our first response in the face of our enemies is often pragmatic. Will forgiveness work? Is it practical? What if racist Mike did not change? Doesn't it just let enemies get away with evil? This is probably why we might dig passages like the whip-wielding Jesus, flipping over tables, drop-kicking cash registers, and employing righteous anger to stop evil. It's a jarring image. But the reason it is so jarring is the exact same reason it shouldn't be a default excuse for angry outbursts: it was out of character for Jesus.

This was not a temper tantrum.[18] The kind of behavior Jesus displayed in the temple that afternoon isn't by any means forbidden, but it wasn't exactly a daily part of Jesus' life, either. Jesus did not walk around with a whip in His back pocket, ready to unleash His rage, as we walk around with our smartphones prepared to light someone up.

This face-off that Jesus displays in the temple was not an outburst; it was more like performance art. In fact, when Jesus overturned the tables, He was reenacting Jeremiah's threat of the coming destruction of the temple (Jer. 19).

Jesus is literally performing. He was not flogging people; the text never states that. He was shooing out the animals with the whip, overturning tables to scatter the doves and coins. This is a public display. There's a vast of difference between attacking one's enemies—which Jesus spoke against—and Jesus' actions in the temple.[19]

Is there space for this kind of public display in the face of injustice or unrighteousness? I think so. Can a nativity scene depicting Joseph, Mary, and baby Jesus as modern immigrants provoke people to rethink their treatment of them?[20] Can a public display of protestors sitting in front of an abortion clinic provoke people to rethink their treatment of babies in the womb? There is a place for protest; Jesus showed us there was.

THE AGE OF OUTRAGE

I wonder though if we have more hope in public outrage. Do we think table-flipping can accomplish more than affection can? Outrage has more momentum than ever thanks in part to social media platforms that allow people to share their reactions quickly and effortlessly. In an age of twenty-four-hour news cycles, the issues can range from coffee cups to war atrocities. On the face of it, the willingness to express outrage could reflect an underlying concern for morality or justice. When MTV aired the first few episodes of Bevis and Butt-Head in the '90s, conservative Christians publicly displayed outrage by starting petitions and pledging to junk their TVs by placing them out on the curb for trash pickup. In 2014, when Hobby Lobby won a Supreme Court decision that allowed their company to exempt certain contraceptives from employees' medical insurance, thousands of progressive protesters gathered at their stores across the country attempting to put them out of business.

Researchers have found that outrage is more an act of self-expression, to signal our virtues to the public.[21] Psychologically, we outrage more to be seen than to seek substantial change. Much of the activism from both conservatives and progressives are more subconsciously a desire to be seen by others as morally upright (conservatives) or socially informed (progressives). Outrage helps us establish our moral standing in the cosmos of our peers.

We feel a catharsis as we rally around our outrage online, in our conversations, or in opposing our enemies. Does calling out people online really help us? Should you practice outrage catharsis?

The theory of catharsis is widespread—that venting one's anger will produce a positive improvement in one's emotional state. The word *catharsis* comes from the Greek word *katharsis*, which literally translated means purging.[22] According to Catharsis Theory, acting aggressively is an effective way to deal with anger. Sigmund Freud started this idea, believing that repressed negative emotions could build up inside an individual and cause psychological damage. He proposed that we needed to discharge our anger to be emotionally healthy. Freud believed venting would get anger "out of your system," therefore decreasing aggression in people.[23] Is this true?

As soon as psychology researchers began conducting scientific tests on Catharsis Theory it's foundations were shaken. In one research test, an aggressive and insulting remark was given to each individual that participated in a group experiment. Only half of the group participants were instructed to pound nails for ten minutes. The other half were not given the same instruction, not getting a chance to vent their anger after being insulted.[24] Freud's theory was exposed; the opposite effect was occurring. Those who had pounded the nails were more hostile, rather than less hostile, than the ones who did not get to pound the nails. We are taught that this type of unleashing of outrage is empowering.

Courtesy of Facebook, the action that you perform with your computer mouse provides you a release, a substitute for the work of love. The striking thing about all electronic devices and applications is that they're designed to be immensely easy. Outrage has nothing on the power of affectionate-action.

Turning the other cheek is active, disrupting the enemy dynamic.

Removing the tunic is active, disrupting the enemy dynamic.

Going the extra mile is active, disrupting the enemy dynamic.

Who do you need to move toward in forgiveness?

THE BURNING COALS

Neuroscience has proven that pummeling your ideological enemy with factoids and arguments will *not* change your enemy's mind. Shauna's practices toward Mike and each of the three Jesus-practices of forgiveness go far beyond tossing information; they give space for the wrongdoer to feel something different, to see us no longer as their enemy, but as a human. Jesus' kenotic-love did not demand reciprocity, it did not seek to control the outcomes, but it did seek to affectionately win us over, to make friends of those opposed to Him.

"If your enemy is hungry, feed him; if he is thirsty, give him something to drink. In doing this, you will heap burning coals on his head" (Rom. 12:20). Here the apostle Paul is giving us some guidance for those who are hardheaded. As we read this, one portion sticks out: "heap burning coals" on an enemy's head. What did he mean by this?

At first read, dumping coals on a person's head sounds like a fight sequence out of a Jason Bourne flick—it's an audacious move. The most dramatic picture we have of burning coals touching our body comes from Isaiah 6:5–7:

> "Woe to me!" I cried. "I am ruined! For I am a man of unclean lips. . . .
>
> Then one of the seraphim flew to me with a live coal in his hand, which he had taken with tongs from the altar. With it he touched my mouth and said, "See, this has touched your lips; your guilt is taken away and your sin atoned for."

This is an act of mercy, of God's initiative to ease Isaiah of his anxiety in God's presence. God, in essence, is saying, "You've done a lot of things that have offended Me, stuff you probably can't even recall, but I forgive you, I want to be near you." These coals are a symbol of God's preemptive forgiveness, an action of God to be near us, with us, close to us.

The coals in this passage are placed on Isaiah's lips because he has *already* verbalized his wrongs ("Woe is me!"). The coals Paul speaks of in Romans of are placed on the head, *not* on the mouth—the hardness of the head vs. the openness of the mouth. This act of forgiveness (heaping hot coals) isn't given to one who asks for it; they might actually be closed off to it. Heaping hot coals is not lambasting someone on social media. It is not arguing with your mother on Facebook. The passage about heaping hot coals on the head is about the emotional discomfort an enemy will experience when you waken their conscience through affection; when they feel kindness in the face of their meanness. We cannot manipulate someone's response. We can only heap hot coals on their head hoping that they feel the love.

Reflection Questions

1. How does the act of forgiveness shift the power between people?

2. How do you know when it's time to just heap hot coals on someone's head?

3. What practical step can you take to practice the aikido of forgiveness with someone?

CONCLUSION

In the Harry Potter books, Harry, Ron, and Hermione are three friends on a journey to overcome evil and restore good to its proper place in the world. Their pilgrimage, like most spiritual journeys, includes one trial after another. In the *Harry Potter and the Sorcerer's Stone* movie, they seek the stone that is the key to the triumph of love and the casting out of fear. To reach the stone, they must overcome a variety of obstacles. The fierce three-headed dog guarding the stone is after them, and they save themselves by jumping through a trap door. They land on something soft, a giant plant, thinking they are out of harm's way.

Suddenly with horror, they feel the plant coiling around them and strangling them. Hermione remembers this plant is called "the devil's snare." The more they fight it, the more the plant closes around them. With every aggressive move, they get bound even more tightly, and their range of motion gets smaller. They panic and struggle harder. The plant closes in even tighter. The more fear they feel, the more trapped they become. Hermione remembers what to do. The solution is to be still. Relax, stop fighting, stop struggling, trust that stillness is the way to loosen this plant's stronghold. With Hermione's guidance, Harry is able to do this. Ron, however, cannot find his way out of his fear.

"There is no fear in love, but perfect love casts out fear" (1 John 4:18 ESV). This truth is a proclamation not to get caught in the devil's snare, the suffocating powers of polarization. The future of the church needs a revolution of love, a love so scandalous it relaxes in the face of fear to move toward enemies with affection.

Do you remember that blistering email sent to me, the one that called me a LIAR? Oh, I do; it still stings a bit. I'm grateful my wife told me to slow down on firing off a defensive email. In my journey to befriend my enemies, I'm learning to pay attention to my immediate reactions and question them. After some stillness and prayer, I knew God was inviting me into the depths of *affection*. How could I do this? Well, I knew my "frenemy" loved wine and fancy cheeses.

In trembling fear, I pieced together a gift basket for him, and planned on delivering it to his house. Every item chosen for that basket brought to mind his face and his vicious words. Yet at the same time, I had to pick things with care and thoughtfulness. I had to imagine what he might enjoy. It was a wild exercise in the paradox of feeling fear and feeling love. It took me a week to put that enemy-love basket together, and by the end, my thoughts about him morphed into something unusual. Sure, I still felt angst inside, but I had a new neuron firing in my brain that said, "You know Dan, he's just like you, hurt, and not knowing how to deal with it."

That drive to his house felt like walking on a bed of nails; it was excruciating. I rehearsed my words, but they all sounded like a defensive four-year-old talking. I knocked on his door, and he answered. Like a deer in the headlights, he wanted to run away. I blurted out, "Before you say anything, I just want to give you this gift; I made it for you, I really care about you, I know you love wine and cheese." His hands didn't move from his pants pockets; he wasn't sure how to receive the gift.

Silence that felt as long as The Lord of the Rings films was snapped. "Come on in, I guess we can talk." We talked at his kitchen table for two plus hours. Our antagonism was slowly unwound, and we both saw how our actions were perceived by the other. We still disagreed on some details, but we forgave each other. The Spirit met us in that exchange of moving beyond attacking or avoiding. We reached for affection, and we found some.

Does every movement of enemy-love bud fruit like this? Well . . . no. That is not the point of befriending our enemies. The point is that we have for the most part taken it off the table, we've lost imagination for healing. Our politics, our churches, and our personal relationships have surrendered to the powers and principalities of polarization. I believe God's kingdom wants to disrupt our side-taking tendencies. We need to park our excuses, get a vision for Jesus, and move toward each other with holy affection. The Enemy wants us to fall into his snare. Love casts out fear. Sit still with this, then grab a few friends, and help them get free. After that, go love your enemies together.

ACKNOWLEDGMENTS

I am so grateful to Duane Sherman (Acquisitions Editor) for believing in the peculiar message of this book. When I said "I want to write a book that slightly irritates both conservatives and progressives," you didn't flinch, and I knew you'd handle this project with care. As well, this book would be a tough read without Connor Sterchi's (Managing Editor) meticulous edits and thoughtful feedback.

Thanks Kevin Max for dwelling with the message of *Love over Fear* and writing a meaningful manifesto in "Be Love." Your art has inspired me over the years. This song is a gift to the revolution of love we are trying to spark.

Thank you, JR Woodward (coconspirator at The V3 Movement), for the stimulating conversations about this book. Your challenging questions sharpened my thinking.

It would be near impossible for me to write this book without the folks in my Christian community and the characters in my neighborhood. The hard work of enemy-love was forged in the fires of both of these domains.

Thank you, Aaron Metthe (coplanter at Axiom), for walking with me through the ups and downs of learning to follow Jesus more closely. We've taken big risks together, and they have changed us to look more like love.

Thanks to Salt City Coffee (my local neighborhood coffee shop) for the dark roast and the warm environment that hosted my writing madness.

Thank you, Tonya (my wife), for the long conversations in the car as we hashed out what God has taught us through our pain. We've wrestled with anger, sadness, and cynicism in the face of attacks, but the Spirit has always pulled us toward healing.

NOTES

Chapter 1: The Way Fear Works

1. Robin L. Snipes, Michael S. LaTour, and Sara J. Bliss, "A Model of the Effects of Self-efficacy on the Perceived Ethicality and Performance of Fear Appeals in Advertising," *Journal of Business Ethics* 19 (April 1999) 273–85.

2. "FDA 2016 Decision and History," Beyond Pesticides, https://www .beyondpesticides.org/programs/antibacterials/triclosan/fda-2016-decision-and-history.

3. Kristen Ulmer, *The Art of Fear: Why Conquering Fear Won't Work and What to Do Instead* (New York: Harper Wave, 2017), 34–36.

4. Tom Pyszczynski, "What Are We So Afraid Of?: A Terror Management Theory Perspective on the Politics of Fear," *Social Research: An International Quarterly* 71, no. 4 (Winter 2004).

5. Shanto Iyengar and Sean J. Westwood, "Fear and Loathing across Party Lines: New Evidence on Group Polarization," *Journal of Political Science* 59 (2015): 690–707.

6. Pyszczynski, "What Are We So Afraid Of?"

7. Politico Staff, "Full text: Donald Trump 2016 RNC draft speech transcript," July 21, 2016, Politico, https://www.politico.com/story/2016/07/full-transcript-donald-trump-nomination-acceptance-speech-at-rnc-225974.

8. Quoted in Mark Leibovich, "'I'm the Last Thing Standing Between You and the Apocalypse,'" *The New York Times*, October 16, 2016, https://www.nytimes.com/2016/10/16/magazine/hillary-clinton-campaign-final-weeks.html.

9. Kristen Ulmer, *The Art of Fear: Why Conquering Fear Won't Work and What to Do Instead* (New York: Harper Wave, 2017), 34–36.

10. Dan White Jr., "The Psychological Junk-Food: Cynicism," *Dan White Jr.* (blog), March 19, 2012, http://danwhitejr.blogspot.com/2012/03/psychological-junk-food-cynicism.html.

11. Ronald Rolheiser, *Forgotten Among the Lilies* (New York: Double Day, 2003), 112–13.

12. Ibid.

13. Ibid.

14. Sendhil Mullainathan, *Scarcity: The Science of Having Less and How It Defines Our Lives* (London: Picador, 2014), 56–58.

15. Robb Rutledge, "A Computational and Neural Model of Happiness," Robb Rutledge (website), August 8, 2014,. https://www.robbrutledge .com/news/2014/8/8/a-computational-and-neural-model-of-happiness.

16. Mullainathan, *Scarcity*, 56–58.

17. Dan White Jr., *Subterranean: Why the Future of the Church is Rootedness* (Eugene, OR: Cascade Books, 2015), 95.

18. Sasha Abramsky, *Jumping at Shadows: The Triumph of Fear and the End of the American Dream* (New York: Nation Books, 2017), 109–110.

19. Ibid.

20. Joshua Greene, *Moral Tribes: Emotion, Reason, and the Gap between Us and Them* (London, England: Penguin Publishing, 2013), 46–48.

21. Gregory Boyd, *Repenting of Religion: Turning From Judgment to the Love of God* (Ada, MI: Baker Books, 2004), 74–75.

Chapter 2: Love and Fear at War

1. *Star Wars: Episode I – The Phantom Menace*, directed by George Lucas (San Francisco: Lucasfilm, 1999).

2. David G. Benner, *Surrender to Love: Discovering the Heart of Christian Spirituality* (Downers Grove, IL: IVP Books, 2003), 22–23.

3. Ibid.

4. Doug Frank, *A Gentler God: Breaking Free of the Almighty in the Company of the Human Jesus* (Menangle, Australia: Albatross, 2010), 133–34.

5. Anthony W. Bartlett, *Seven Stories: How to Study and Teach the Nonviolent Bible* (Syracuse, NY: Hopetime Press, 2017), 46–48.

6. Stuart Murray, *The Naked Anabaptist: The Bare Essential of a Radical Faith* (Scottdale, PA: Herald Press, 2010), 88–90.

7. Hans Urs Von Balthassar, *Love Alone is Credible* (San Francisco: Ignatius Press, 1963), 91–92.

8. Ibid.

9. Karl Barth, *The Doctrine of God: Church Dogmatics, Vol. 2, Part 1* (Edinburgh, Scotland: T&T Clark, 1957), 157–59.

10. Lee C. Camp, *Mere Discipleship: Radical Christianity in a Rebellious World* (Grand Rapids: Brazos Press, 2003), 26–27.

11. *Bede's Ecclesiastical History of the English People*, ed. Bertram Colgrave and R. A. B. Mynors. (Oxford: Clarendon Press, 1968), 150–51.

12. Von Balthassar, *Love Alone Is Credible*, 92–93.
13. Mike Bennett, "Fear of the Lord: What Does It Mean?," Life, Hope & Truth, https://lifehopeandtruth.com/god/who-is-god/fear-of-the-lord/.
14. Brennan Manning, *Abba's Child: The Cry of the Heart for Intimate Belonging* (Colorado Springs: NavPress, 2002), 20.
15. Søren Kierkegaard, *Fear and Trembling* (1843; repr., London: Penguin Books, 1985), 52–53.
16. Reuven Hammer, *The Classic Midrash: Tannaitic Commentaries on the Bible* (Mahwah, NJ: Pualist, 1995), 190–91.
17. Ibid.
18. Scot McKnight, *Embracing Grace: A Gospel for All of Us* (Orleans, MA: Paraclete Press, 2012), 42–43.
19. Robin Dunbar, *Grooming, Gossip, and the Evolution of Language* (Cambridge, MA: Harvard University Press, 1998), 132–33.
20. Anthony W. Bartlett, *Seven Stories: How to Study and Teach the Nonviolent Bible* (Syracuse, NY: Hopetime Press, 2017), 62–64.

Chapter 3: How Fear Polarizes Us

1. Basing this off the traditional fight-or-flight response (also called acute stress response) is a physiological reaction that occurs in response to a perceived harmful event to survival. It was first described by Walter Bradford Cannon in his book *The Wisdom of the Body*, 1932.
2. Michael J. Gorman, *Reading Revelation Responsibly: Uncivil Worship and Witness: Following the Lamb into the New Creation* (Eugene, OR: Wipf & Stock, 2011), 78–81.
3. Ibid.
4. Tim Gombis, "Describing Passive-Aggressive Relational Postures," *Faith Improvised* (blog), August 3, 2012, https://timgombis.com/2012/08/03/describing-passive-aggressive-relational-postures.
5. Ibid.
6. Thank you Giles Sieburg (clinical therapist) for our conversations on neurology and trauma.
7. Dan White Jr., "When Clinton and Bush Go to Church . . .Together," V3, January 23, 2017, http://thev3movement.org/2017/01/when-clinton-and-bush-go-to-church/.
8. Walter Wink, *Engaging the Powers: Discernment and Resistance in a World of Domination* (Minneapolis: Fortress, 1992), 95–98.
9. Joshua Greene, *Moral Tribes: Emotion, Reason, and the Gap Between Us and Them* (London, England: Penguin Publishing, 2013), 112–14.
10. Ibid.

11. Robin Dunbar, *The Science of Love* (New York: Wiley, 2012), 92–93.

12. Jonathan Haidt, *The Righteous Mind: Why Good People Are Divided by Politics and Religion* (New York: Random House, 2012), 145–46.

13. Carl Jung, *The Development of Personality*, The Collected Works of C. G. Jung, vol. 17 (Princeton: Princeton University Press, 1954), 135–36.

14. Ibid.

15. Wil Hernandez, *Henri Nouwen and Spiritual Polarities: A Life of Tension* (Mahwah, NJ: Paulist Press, 2012), 85–87.

16. "False Dilemma Examples," SoftSchools.com, http://www.softschools.com/examples/fallacies/false_dilemma_examples/491/.

17. Ibid.

18. Ibid.

19. "Logical Fallacies," Flashcards, Quizlet, https://quizlet.com/40675962/logical-fallacies-flash-cards/.

20. Carl Jung, *The Structure and Dynamics of the Psyche*, The Collected Works of C. G. Jung, vol. 8 (Princeton: Princeton University Press, 1960) 133–134.

21. David Ropeik, "How Tribalism Overrules Reason, and Makes Risky Times More Dangerous," Big Think, May 14, 2012, http://bigthink.com/risk-reason-and-reality/how-tribalism-overrules-reason-and-makes-risky-times-more-dangerous.

22. Shaye J.D. Cohen, Paula Fredriksen, and L. Michael White, "Judaism's First Century Diversity," PBS, April 1998, https://www.pbs.org/wgbh/pages/frontline//////shows/religion/portrait/judaism.html.

23. Josephus Flavius, *The Works of Josephus: Complete and Unabridged, New Updated Edition* (Peabody, MA: Hendrickson, 1980), 235–39.

24. Cohen, Fredriksen, and White, "Judaism's First Century Diversity."

25. Flavius, *The Works of Josephus*, 235–39.

26. Ibid.

27. Josephus Flavius, *The Jewish War* (Peabody, MA: Hendrickson, 1980), 201–203. Many first-century historians believe Judas's surname Iscariot was a corruption of the Latin *sicarius* ("murderer" or "assassin") rather than an indication of family origin; Josephus establishes that Sicarii was a radical Jewish group, some of whom were terrorists. This has become a commonly held sociohistorical belief in the last fifteen years or so.

28. Matthew Murray, *The Sons of Zebedee: A Biography of the Apostle James and John* (Buchanan, NY: BookCaps, 2013), 45–52.

29. Joe Iovino, "Living As a Person of Peace in a Broken World," UMC.org, http://www.umc.org/what-we-believe/living-as-a-person-of-peace-in-a-broken-world.

Chapter 4: Affection for Monsters

1. Damien Kempf and Maria Gilbert, *Medieval Monsters* (London: British Library, 2015), 135–39.

2. Ibid.

3. Jean Vanier and Stanley Hauerwas, *Living Gently in a Violent World: The Prophetic Witness of Weakness* (Downers Grove, IL: IVP Books, 2018), 62–63.

4. E. Stanley Jones, *The Unshakable Kingdom and the Unchanging Person* (New York: McNett Press, 1995), 135–36.

5. Tim Suttle, "Stanley Hauerwas: A Prayer for Our Enemies As We Are All Learning How to Hate," October 19, 2017, http://www.patheos .com/blogs/paperbacktheology/2017/10/stanley-hauerwas-prayer-enemies-learning-hate.html.

6. Ibid.

7. Wayne Gordon, *Who Is My Neighbor?: Lessons Learned from a Man Left for Dead* (Ventura, CA: Gospel Light, 2010), 133–34.

8. Ibid.

9. Wendell Berry, *It All Turns on Affection: The Jefferson Lecture and Other Essays* (Berkeley, CA: Counterpoint Press, 2012).

10. Tim Suttle, "Stanley Hauerwas: A Prayer for Our Enemies as We Are All Learning How to Hate," October 19, 2017, http://www.patheos .com/blogs/paperbacktheology/2017/10/stanley-hauerwas-prayer-enemies-learning-hate.html.

11. David Benjamin Blower, *Sympathy for Jonah: Reflections on Humiliation, Terror and the Politics of Enemy-Love* (Eugene, OR: Wipf & Stock, 2014), 44–48.

12. Ibid.

13. Ibid.

14. Sara H. Konrath, Edward H. O'Brien, and Courtney Hsing, "Changes in Dispositional Empathy in American College Students Over Time: A Meta-Analysis," *Personality and Social Psychology Review* 15, no. 2 (2010).

15. Ibid.

16. Phyllis Tickle, *The Great Emergence: How Christianity Is Changing and Why* (Grand Rapids: Baker Books, 2008), 115–16.

17. Janna Anderson and Lee Rainie, "The Future of Well-Being in a Tech-Saturated World," Pew Research Center, http://www.elon.edu/ docs/e-web/imagining/surveys/2018_survey/Elon_Pew_Digital _Life_and_Well_Being_Report_2018_Expanded_Version.pdf; "Political Polarization in the American Public," Pew Research Center, June 12, 2014, http://www.people-press.org/2014/06/12/

political-polarization-in-the-american-public/; Dan White Jr., "When Clinton and Bush Go to Church . . . Together," V3, January 23, 2017, http://thev3movement.org/2017/01/when- clinton-and-bush-go-to-church/.

18. "U.S. Adults Have Few Friends—and They're Mostly Alike," Barna Trends 2018, October 23, 2018, https://www.barna.com/research/friends-loneliness/.

19. Mallory Simon and Sara Sidner, "What Happened When a Klansman Met a Black Man in Charlottesville," CNN, updated December 16, 2017, https://www.cnn.com/2017/12/15/us/charlottesville-klansman-black-man-meeting/index.html. "How One Man Convinced 200 Ku Klux Klan Members to Give Up Their Robes," *All Things Considered*, August 20, 2017, https://www.npr.org/2017/08/20/544861933/how-one-man-convinced-200-ku-klux-klan-members-to-give-up-their-robes.

20. Simon and Sidner, "What Happened When a Klansman Met a Black Man in Charlottesville."

21. Ibid.

22. Ibid.

23. Martin Luther King Jr., "An Address by the Reverend Dr. Martin Luther King, Jr." (speech, Cornell College, Mount Vernon, Iowa, October 15, 1962), Cornell College, https://news.cornellcollege.edu/dr-martin-luther-kings-visit-to-cornell-college/.

24. Richard Beck, *Unclean: Meditations on Purity, Hospitality, and Mortality* (Eugene, OR: Cascade Books, 2011), 77–79.

Chapter 5: When Love Comes to Town

1. David Benjamin Blower, *Sympathy for Jonah: Reflections on Humiliation, Terror and the Politics of Enemy-Love* (Eugene, OR: Wipf & Stock, 2014), 95–98.

2. Lorraine Devon Wilke, "Deconstructing the Expert Delusion: No, Not Everyone Is One," *Huffington Post*, December 6, 2017, https://www.huffingtonpost.com/lorraine-devon-wilke/deconstructing-the-expert-delusion_b_4735182.html.

3. Peter Senge, *The Fifth Discipline: The Art and Practice of Learning* (New York: Random House, 1999), 35–39.

4. René Descartes, *Descartes: The Essential Collection* (New York: Titan Read, 2014), 144–46.

5. Ibid.

6. P. J. Manney, "Is Technology Destroying Empathy?," Live Science, June 30, 2015, https://www.livescience.com/51392-will-tech-bring-humanity-together-or-tear-it-apart.html.

7. Joseph Burgo, *The Narcissist You Know: Defending Yourself Against Extreme Narcissists* (New York: Touchstone, 2015), 122–23.

8. Michela Del Vicario et al., "The Spreading of Misinformation Online," *Proceedings of the National Academy of Sciences* 113, no. 3 (January 2016).

9. Ann Jervis, *Paul: Ethics in the Ancient Mediterranean World* (Princeton, NJ: Princeton University, 2001), 35–39.

10. Homer, *Iliad* (Book I), eNotes, https://www.enotes.com/topics/iliad/text/book-i.

11. Esther Lightcap Meek, *Loving to Know: Covenant Epistemology* (Eugene, OR: Wipf & Stock, 2011), 205–207.

12. Ibid.

13. Sasha Abramsky, *Jumping at Shadows: The Triumph of Fear and the End of the American Dream* (New York: Nation Books, 2017), 25–28.

14. Michael Shermer, "How to Convince Someone When Facts Fail," Scientific American, January 1, 2017, https://www.scientificamerican.com/article/how-to-convince-someone-when-facts-fail/.

15. Brendan Nyhan and Jason Reifler. "When Corrections Fail: The Persistence of Political Misperceptions," *Political Behavior* 32, no. 2 (June 2010).

16. Ibid.

17. Marnie Eisenstadt, "Friendship Formed in Disagreement. One Wants Better Gun Control, One Supports the NRA," Syracuse.com, April 6, 2018, https://www.syracuse.com/living/index.ssf/2018/04/a_friendship_forged_in_disagreement_one_wants_better_gun_control_one_supports_th.html.

18. Ibid.

19. Marcus Peter Rempel, *Life at the End of Us Vs. Them: Cross Cultural Stories* (Victoria, BC: Friesen Press, 2017) 120–123.

20. David Benjamin Blower, *Sympathy for Jonah: Reflections on Humiliation, Terror and the Politics of Enemy-Love* (Eugene, OR: Wipf & Stock, 2014) 65–67.

21. "The Four Loves," Wikipedia, last edited November 18, 2018, https://en.wikipedia.org/wiki/The_Four_Loves.

22. Richard Rohr, *The Art of Letting Go: Living the Wisdom of Saint Francis.* https://cac.org/the-path-of-descent-2017-06-21/.

23. Richard Beck, *Unclean: Meditations on Purity, Hospitality, and Mortality* (Eugene, OR: Cascade Books, 2011) 115–116.

24. Ibid.

25. David Benjamin Blower, *Sympathy for Jonah,* 67–69.

26. Kallistos Ware, *The Orthodox Way*, rev. ed. (Crestwood, NY: St Vladimir's Seminary Press, 1995), 69–72.

27. John Howard Yoder, *The Politics of Jesus* (Grand Rapids: Eerdmans, 1994), 90–92.

Chapter 6: Breaking Open Space

1. David Fitch, "Neither Do I Condemn Thee: Making Space for Alternative Sexualities in Our Midst," Missio Alliance, November 10, 2015, https://www.missioalliance.org/neither-condemn-thee-making-space-alternative-sexualities-midst/.

2. "Mens Rea," Legal Information Institute, https://www.law.cornell.edu/wex/mens_rea.

3. "Chapter 8– The Federal Courts: The Judicial Branch," Flashcards, Quizlet, https://quizlet.com/111803820/chapter-8-the-federal-courts-the-judicial-branch-flash-cards/.

4. Gayle Olson-Raymer, "The Role of the Federal Government in Juvenile Delinquency Prevention: Historical and Contemporary Perspectives," *Journal of Criminal Law and Criminology* 74, no. 2 (Summer 1983).

5. Dietrich Bonhoeffer, *Ethics*, trans. N. H. Smith (New York: Simon & Schuster, 1949) 111–14.

6. Robert V. Wolf, "Highlights of a Roundtable Discussion among Tribal and State Leaders," Center for Court Innovation, http://www.courtinnovation.org/sites/default/files/documents/Peacemaking_Today.pdf.

7. Ibid.

8. Tadodaho Sid Hill, "Tadodaho Sid Hill speaks with Renee K. Gadoua," YouTube, https://www.youtube.com/watch?v=4NaX0lA3S50. I learned many of these principles from Onondaga Nations leader Tadodaho Sid Hill.

9. David E. Garland, "The Dispute Over Food Sacrificed to Idols," https://www.vanderbilt.edu/AnS/religious_studies/SNTS2002/garland.htm.

10. Ibid.

11. Ibid.

12. N. T. Wright, *1 Corinthians: N.T. Wright for Everyone Bible Study Guides* (London: SPCK Publishing, 2003), 165–67.

13. Dietrich Bonhoeffer, *Ethics*, trans. N. H. Smith (New York: Simon & Schuster, 1949), 112–14.

14. Peter Kreeft, *Knowing the Truth of God's Love: The One Thing We Can't Live Without* (Ann Arbor, MI: Servant Press, 1988), 84–86.

15. Larry Crabb, *Connecting: Healing for Ourselves and Our Relationships* (Nashville: Word, 1997), 75–76.

16. Ibid.

17. Fitch, "Neither Do I Condemn Thee."

18. Ibid.

19. Thank you Terri Pease from The Park Church San Antonio for sharing this story with me.

Chapter 7: Making Meals for Frenemies

1. Michael J. McVicar, "The Religious Right in America," Oxford Research Encyclopedias, http://oxfordre.com/religion/view/10.1093/acrefore/9780199340378.001.0001/acrefore-9780199340378-e-97.

2. Jim Wallis, "The New Evangelical Leaders, Part I," interview by Krista Tippett, *On Being with Krista Tippett*, November 29, 2007, https://onbeing.org/programs/jim-wallis-the-new-evangelical-leaders-part-i/.

3. Jedediah Purdy, "North Carolina's Long Moral March and Its Lessons for the Trump Resistance," *The New Yorker*, February 17, 2017, https://www.newyorker.com/news/news-desk/north-carolinas-long-moral-march-and-its-lessons-for-the-trump-resistance.

4. Marcus Peter Rempel, *Life at the End of Us vs. Them: Cross Cultural Stories* (Victoria, BC: FriesenPress, 2017), 130–32.

5. CT Editors, "What Tim Keller Wants American Christians to Know about Politics," *Christianity Today*, October 3, 2018, https://www.christianitytoday.com/ct/2018/october-web-only/tim-keller-politics-news-midterms-united-states.html.

6. Mark Glanville, "Jesus Ate His Way through the Gospels….," Westville Presby Presbyterian Church, July 28, 2017, https://www.westvillepresby.co.za/2017/07/28/jesus-ate-his-way-through-the-gospels/.

7. Jan Michael Joncas, "Tasting the Reign of God: The Meal Ministry of Jesus and Its Implications for Christian Worship and Life" (Habiger Lecture, St. Paul, MN, April 10, 2000), 114–17.

8. Ibid.

9. Ibid.

10. "The Revolutionary Table of Jesus," Lutheran Campus Ministry in Baltimore, September 2, 2013, https://www.baltimorelutherancampus-ministry.org/apps/blog/show/32736062-the-revolutionary-table-of-jesus.

11. Lisa Hickman, "Eating with the Enemy: Esther's Story," HuffPost, September 26, 2012, updated December 6, 2017, https://www.huffingtonpost.com/lisa-hickman/eating-with-the-enemy-est_b_1916776.html.

12. Ibid.

13. Marva J. Dawn, *Powers, Weakness, and the Tabernacling of God* (Grand Rapids: Eerdmans, 2001), 94–97.

14. C. S. Lewis, *The Weight of Glory* (San Francisco, CA: HarperOne, 1977), 122–23.

15. Leanne Payne, *Real Presence: The Glory of Christ With Us and Within Us* (Grand Rapids: Baker Books, 1979), 114–16.

16. Greg Paul, *God in the Alley: Being and Seeing Jesus in a Broken World* (Colorado Springs: Watebrook Press, 2004), 74–75.

17. John Howard Yoder, *The Politics of Jesus* (Grand Rapids: Eerdmans, 1994), 111–13.

18. Jon Huckins and Rob Yackley, *Thin Places: 6 Postures for Creating and Practicing Missional Community* (Kansas City, MO: The House Studio, 2012), 74–77.

19. Susha Roberts, "10 Lessons from Jesus' Table," Wycliffe, https://www.wycliffe.org/feast/10-lessons-from-jesus-table.

20. Marnie Eisenstadt, "He Once Ate Out of Garbage Cans and Sold Drugs, Now He's Feeding Syracuse's Homeless," December 11, 2017, updated July 20, 2018, https://www.syracuse.com/living/index.ssf/2017/12/he_once_ate_out_of_garbage_cans_and_sold_drugs_now_hes_feeding_syracuses_homeles.html.

21. Ibid.

22. Aaron Chambers, *Eats with Sinner: Loving Like Jesus* (Colorado Springs: NavPress, 2009), 41–43.

Chapter 8: Compassionate Curiosity

1. Abraham Cohen, *Everyman's Talmud: The Major Teachings of the Rabbinic Sages* (New York: BN Publishing, 2008), 84–86.

2. William Packer, *Narratives of a Vulnerable God* (London, England: John Knox, 1994), 64–66.

3. Mario Livio, *Why?: What Makes Us Curious* (New York: Simon & Schuster, 2017), 111–12.

4. Ibid.

5. Ibid.

6. Adrian F. Ward, "The Neuroscience of Everybody's Favorite Topic," Scientific American, July 16, 2013, https://www.scientificamerican.com/article/the-neuroscience-of-everybody-favorite-topic-themselves/.

7. Scot McKnight, *A Fellowship of Differents: Showing the World God's Design for Life Together* (Grand Rapids: Zondervan, 2015), 44–47.

8. Vicky Hartley, "The Secret to Being Present in a Conversation," Watkins, September 26, 2016, https://www.watkinspublishing.com/the-secret-to-being-present-in-a-conversation/.

9. Brian D. McLaren, *The Secret Message of Jesus* (Nashville: Thomas Nelson, 2006), 113–14.

10. Slavoj Zizek, *The Sublime Object of Ideology* (Brooklyn, NY: Verso Press, 2009), 89–92.

11. Peter Block, *Community: The Structure of Belonging* (San Francisco: Berret-Koehler, 2008), 120–22.

Chapter 9: The Aikido of Forgiveness

1. Sarah Lewis, *The Rise: Creativity, the Gift of Failure, and the Search for Mastery* (New York: Simon & Schuster, 2015), 70–73.

2. Ibid.

3. Wendy Palmer, *The Practice of Freedom: Aikido Principles as a Spiritual Guide and The Intuitive Body* (Boulder, CO: Rodmell Press, 2010), 34–35.

4. Ibid.

5. Ibid.

6. Stanley Hauerwas, *Matthew*, Brazos Theological Commentary on the Bible (Grand Rapids: Brazos, 2006), 67–68.

7. Glen H. Stassen, *Living the Sermon on the Mount* (San Francisco: Jossey-Bass, 2006), 82–84.

8. Ibid.

9. Ibid.

10. Josephus Flavius, *The Works of Josephus: Complete and Unabridged, New Updated Edition* (Peabody, MA: Hendrickson Pub, 1980), 222‑23.

11. Hauerwas, *Matthew*, 132–33.

12. Christopher Kaczor, *The Gospel of Happiness: Rediscovery Your Faith through Spiritual Practices* (New York: Crown Publishing, 2015), 71–72.

13. Ibid.

14. Joan O'C Hamilton, "Peace Work," *Stanford Magazine*, May/June 2001, https://stanfordmag.org/contents/peace-work.

15. Fred Luskin, quoted in ibid.

16. Howard Thurman, *Jesus and the Disinherited* (Nashville: Abington Press, 1949), 90–91.

17. See Kaczor, *The Gospel of Happiness*, 71–72.

18. Brad Jersak, "The So-Called 'Violence' of Jesus in the So-Called 'Cleansing of the Temple,'" *Clarion: Journal of Spirituality and Justice*, June 17, 2013, http://www.clarion-journal.com/clarion_journal_of_spirit/2013/06/the-so-called-violence-of-jesus-in-the-so-called-cleansing-of-the-temple-by-brad-jersak.html.

19. Ibid.

20. Matt McKinney, "Indianapolis Church Locks Up Mary, Joseph, Baby Jesus to Condemn Immigration Policy," The Indy Channel, July 3, 2018, https://www.theindychannel.com/news/local-news/

indianapolis/indianapolis-church-locks-up-mary-joseph-baby-jesus-to-condemn-immigration-policy.

21. Zachary K. Rothschild and Lucas A. Keefer, "What Makes People Express Moral Outrage?," *The Guardian*, April 3, 2017, https://www.theguardian.com/commentisfree/2017/apr/03/moral-outrage-public-anger-reasons.

22. Brad J. Bushman, "Does Venting Anger Feed or Extinguish the Flame? Catharsis, Rumination, Distraction, Anger, and Aggressive Responding," *Personality and Social Psychology Bulletin* 28, no. 6 (2002).

23. Ibid.

24. Ibid.